MENTAL ILLNESS

Behind the Smiles and the Tears

A good percentage of this book
will go to mental health

by Margaret Mitchell

M-Y BOOKS PAPERBACK

© Copyright 2016
Margaret Mitchell

A CIP catalogue record for this title is
available from the British Library

ISBN–978-1-911124-29-0

To Stewart,

thank you for
all your help and support

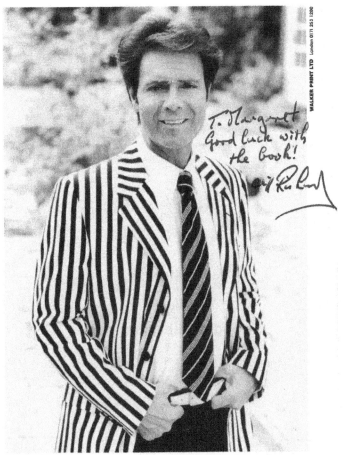

1997 / 43429
© CLIFF RICHARD ORGANISATION - PHOTOGRAPHER: PAUL COX

CLIFF RICHARD

Cliff kindly sent me this signed photograph wishing me luck.

Margaret

IN THE MIND OF MENTAL ILLNESS
Behind the Smiles and the Tears
by Margaret Mitchell

I suffered post-natal depression in 1980 which lead to manic depression - now known as bi-polar.

The book project started back in 1997 at Rainbow Clubhouse. I advertised for sufferers to send me written work and pictures.

Unfortunately many of the organisations mentioned in this book do not exist today in Chelmsford, Essex - and maybe other towns. If this book is successful I want this situation to change. I intend to donate the majority of sales to improve mental health facilities.

Due to my illness it has taken many years to eventually have my book finished and published.

This year (2016) I started attending a Baptist Church and I have had some support. I am grateful to everyone that has encouraged me which has lead to my book finally being published.

The Rainbow Clubhouse has since closed.

CONTENTS

DREAMS CAN COME TRUE

THE BOOK PROJECT by Margaret Mitchell
with help from Rainbow Clubhouse. Interact,
The Dove Centre, The Presbyterian Church. Friends. Family and Associates

I, Margaret Mitchell, have been a sufferer from mental illness since 1980. It all started with post-natal depression and developed into manic depression. There have been many difficult times and I felt that it would be wonderful if I could turn all my suffering into something positive in the form of writing a book. I have always had faith in God, and I felt that my suffering would not all be in vain if I could educate other people about life through my eyes and promote a greater understanding of mental health. In 1997, I joined Rainbow Clubhouse, and they helped me to gain confidence. When I spoke to Jan, the manager at that time, about wanting to write the book she was very enthusiastic about the idea. Wheels have been rolling, and at this point in time I have a very large folder full of material for the book. My dream is becoming a reality.

Birth of book: 23 October 1997

The Rainbow Clubhouse has since closed.

ACKNOWLEDGEMENTS

- Stewart Mitchell
- Ruth Ferguson
- M-Y Books Ltd
- Staff and Members of Chelmsford and District MIND in Chelmsford (formerly known as The Dove Centre)
- Reprohouse
- Linda Cusick
- Jenny Cass
- Richard Peach
- Everyone who has helped with the project
- All those who have contributed pieces of work

29 October 2016

I started this book in 1997! It is now nearly 20 years later. As you will see there are organisations that no longer exist in Chelmsford, Essex. Money allocated to mental health seems to decrease and decrease - more money badly needs to be spent on it. Sufferers are left with next to no support. There is next to nothing to help sufferers cope with life. A non-sufferer often doesn't understand this illness, so sufferers end up suffering on their own with non-sufferers giving little or no support I saw a programme recently about how sufferers were crying out for help and they just didn't receive it, which lead to the sufferer fatally killing someone - how can you blame a sufferer if they do not receive the help they so badly need?

I hope this book is successful and helps to provide money for Mental Health. You sometimes hear of someone with a mental illness attach someone in the newspaper -people seem to blame someone with mental illness - but how can they? It is an illness that probably had not been treated. Mental Health must not be ignored.

Margaret Mitchell

IN THE MIND OF MENTAL ILLNESS
Behind the Smiles and the Tears

Margaret Mitchell and friends 1997

1 Peter 1:6
In this you greatly rejoice, though now for a little while you may
have had to suffer grief in all kinds of trials.

John 14:1
Do not let your hearts be troubled. Trust in God; trust in me.

Corinthians 4:18
So we fix our eyes not on what is seen, but on what is unseen. For
what is seen is temporary, but what is unseen is eternal.

AIMS OF THE BOOK

'IN THE MIND OF MENTAL ILLNESS -
Behind the Smiles and the Tears'

The aim of the book is to have someone come along who doesn't know a lot, or anything at all, about mental illness, and for them to read my book and feel they understand more and become compassionate about sufferers of mental illness and their carers.

INTRODUCTION

19th October 2008

It was 1997, and my husband Stewart and I arrived home from a Cliff Richard concert (it was a charity concert I believe – of course he had to be involved, didn't he?) I turned to Stewart in the car and, after a lot of thought, I mentioned the idea of writing a book about my experiences of mental illness. Stewart said it was okay, so the next day I asked what was then known as The Rainbow Clubhouse about writing the book there. They agreed, and that was the start.

I found myself advertising for people to write to me. I was very fortunate to receive so much mail! It was very encouraging. Time went by, and I found myself becoming ill with manic depression again. I had to put the book aside, and that is the way it went many times.

Later, I moved to doing my book at The Dove Centre (now known as MIND), and then at home.

You must forgive some of the photographs and written work if they are not up to date. This project has taken 11 years so far, and there have been a lot of changes.

Margaret Mitchell

The Dove Centre is no longer in Chelmsford

FOREWORD

I feel very honoured to have been invited to write the foreword to this stimulating book. In my work developing services with NSF to meet the needs of people affected by serious mental health problems, I have been motivated and inspired so often by those people we are seeking to support. People's commitment to help others in the same situation, their resilience, bravery, humour and creativity are what sustain me when the battles with lack of funding, with lack of understanding and above all with stigma seem endless. I have heard the view expressed that mental illness is a manifestation of the evolution of what it is that makes us human, and I think this book demonstrates that admirably. There is something in the creative work of people touched by mental health problems, which seems to reach down (or should that be up) into the very essence of all the qualities that define us as human. It makes essential reading for anyone who regards him or herself a human being.

Erica Lewis
Regional Director,
NSF EasternNSF – National Schizophrenia Fellowship

Please note:

Severalls was the mental health hospital in Colchester. It has since closed. Now there is The Linden Centre, which includes Tillingham Day Hospital in Chelmsford.

The Dove Centre (Chelmsford and District MIND,) was a mental health centre that offered support and activities for people with mental health problems.

The Rainbow Clubhouse was a work-based centre for people with mental health problems.

Millrace IT brings the benefits of Information Technology into everyday life working with disadvantaged people.

Rethink holds activities for people with mental health problems.

20/3/98

THE WORLD ACCORDING TO
MARGARET MITCHELL

Let's start at the very beginning. I was born at an early age on 1st April 1958 (you can tell it's All Fools Day, can't you) at St. Mary's Hospital, Stratford El 5. My mum, dad, brother and I lived with my grandmother for the first three years of my life. We moved to our own home at Chelmsford, Essex (my parents still live there). My brother and I attended the Immaculate Conception Primary and Junior School, where I found learning quite a difficult experience. I had a best friend called Louise, and even today we still keep in touch.

I went to St. John Payne Secondary School, where I still found learning a difficult experience, although I flourished in typing, and I surpassed myself with the geography project I worked on. I made a good friend called Katy (my friend Louise went to a different secondary school). My first experience of mental illness was when Katy became withdrawn and acted strangely. I didn't feel I should ask her any probing questions, I just remained her friend, even though she was a changed person. She was nothing like the friend I had known in the past, but she was still my friend, and being friends means being friends in bad times, as well as in good. We also still keep in touch.

I left school with seven CSE's and one RSA1 in typing. I had several clerical jobs. I met my husband, Stewart, and we married in September, 1978. In June 1980 we had our daughter, Michelle, and that's when I had post-natal depression. This led on to manic depression in 1982. Over the years I have had spells in hospital, but also there have been periods when I have been really well, and even wondering myself why it is that other people could possibly suffer from depression. I even questioned it!

Over the years I have taken up adult education, and gained an RSA1 in Maths and a GCSE grade 2 in English Language. At Inter-Act at The Mill, I obtained a credit in a BTEC in Computer Studies. I found that I really did enjoy it and was able to absorb my studies. Life really can be a joy to live. At these times I can really appreciate how lucky we are to experience good health. It really is a blessing. I guess my favourite achievements have been bringing up my daughter and being able to enjoy a good relationship with my husband, even though times have been tough.

Today I am in good health, if not a bit on the 'high' side just now - so watch out, world!

GLUM

I do feel rather glum,
   I can tell you it's not much fun.
Trying to find an inspiration
   They say that it's 99 per cent perspiration!
Anything would be better than feeling frustrated.
Sitting here feels as if too long I have waited,
Strumming my fingers
   Feelings just linger
Clutching at straws
   Imagination draws
      My mind to thoughts of muddled ambition
        To write a book, I have a vision.

Margaret

1. ILLNESS:

1a How it feels

MANIC DEPRESSION SUFFERER

I suffer from manic depression. People who suffer from manic depression experience 'highs' and 'lows'. When I get high I have an abundance of energy. There are not enough hours in the day to do all the things I want to do. I just want to do everything. My husband becomes very concerned and very worried. I can only interpret this as him becoming annoyed with me, as though he only wants to spoil my fun. When eventually I do calm down, which is usually in hospital, I then discover what the 'lows' are all about. It's hard to explain to people what the lows are about. I find when I am experiencing them that they really are awful. Some people may advise me to do something like bake lots of cakes to make me feel better, but nothing makes you feel better. It's not something you can get out of. It wouldn't be so bad if you knew that from 6 p.m. life would be wonderful, and the rest would be hell, you could then have a few hours when it would all be okay, but it doesn't work like that, it's with you all the time.

Margaret

HI!

I'm going through a 'high', and it's exhausting! I have so much energy and enthusiasm, wanting to do everything that takes my fancy. Re-potting plants, polishing tables, getting rid of cobwebs etcetera etcetera. Not to mention listening to Cliff Richard's music at every possible minute. I am staying up late watching Cliff on video. Yes, I'm a sad person, some people would say! I get the giggles quite a lot too, and I can be silly. I find so many funny angles to what people are saying, I play on words. This is the other me, this is the other extreme I reach. With manic depression you go from a big high to a low low or visa-versa. It's like a pendulum swinging; the higher it goes one way, it will eventually swing the same distance in the other direction. I am keeping in touch with my doctor constantly, hoping to catch this illness and 'nip it in the bud', so that I will very slowly lower myself down to 'normal' rather than crash down to a low. I think it's working; I am sleeping better and feel more in control. Last week I made myself have a week's break from doing this book project, and now I am back! There's nothing stopping me now...

Margaret

DEPRESSION

"I don't want to face the day"

"Leave me alone"

"Don't draw the curtains"

"I want to stay in the dark"

"Nobody understands"

DEPRESSION

It is hard for those who don't suffer from depression to understand what is wrong with someone like me. I have a wonderful family, a nice home and garden. They feel that I have nothing to feel down about. The thing is, the nearest they come to depression is when they feel fed up, and if they are fed up it is quite easy to remedy this by doing something and they know that when they've done it they'll feel better. I can appreciate that as well, but for me depression is much worse than feeling fed up. I know that no matter what I do, it doesn't seem to get better. It is with me 24 hours a day. That is what is so awful about this illness, there is no escape.

People may think I'm weak because I cry and perhaps carry on sometimes - but I feel people like me are strong. We need to be to be able to cope with this illness. It would be weak of me to give up, but I don't. Crying makes it easier, but I still have to face carrying on, getting out of bed, doing the washing up, the ironing, the evening meal. Feeling bad makes all of these things into a nightmare. I can see no end, so I can appreciate some people ending it all. That can seem the only way out of this nightmare, just being dead and 'resting in peace'. Thoughts like that go through every sufferer's mind, and I feel for all of those people who have succeeded in committing suicide. For me I know it is not the answer, I just have to hang on to memories of better times when I am well and I have to remind myself that those days will return.

Some families find it impossible to understand a relative's illness. So if they do not have love and support from their nearest and dearest, and life seems just a downward struggle, how can they possibly be blamed for taking that overdose?

I am lucky to have much love and support from many people, including family, friends and people working within the caring profession. Even so, it is still a struggle sometimes, but I bear with it.

I have a good friend who reminds me that God loves me, and she has sent me some nice cards reminding me of that fact, but, most of all, I own a framed piece called 'Footsteps' that is most comforting. I can feel when I'm going through one of my dark hours that God is with me and that he is carrying me with my burden when I'm at my worst.

I hope with this book, I will be able to help people who do not suffer this awful hell of an illness to be able to have some kind of enlightenment into the life of a sufferer. That is my prayer.

Margaret

26/2/98

SHOULD PEOPLE WHO SUFFER FROM MENTAL ILLNESS HAVE CHILDREN?

I personally have been blessed, as I have a 17-year-old daughter. Looking back, there were many times, especially when my 'daughter was young, that I found it very difficult, as I not only had manic depression, which was hard enough to cope with, but I also had a daughter dependent on me for love and support. Over the years I have found that the joy I feel at times with my daughter overrides any of the times of difficulty I went through as a mother. I feel today I have a wonderful relationship with her. She feels guilt at the fact that it wasn't until I had her that I started to suffer with manic depression. Having her is one of the best things that has happened to me. Even with my illness we have grown close, and in a way she is thankful that she has learnt and had an insight into my world, it has made her a lot more sympathetic towards people who suffer mentally. I feel that over the years my daughter and I have forged a very close relationship that may not have been as close as it is if we hadn't got through all the times when life was difficult for both of us. I have always tried to be a good mother, and have always talked to her about my illness in a way she would have understood, but not in a way to make her feel pressurised, because cutting her out would have been the wrong thing to do. Children need to feel involved with the situation, and I needed to feel she was included in my world without burdening her.

So should people who suffer from mental illness have children or not? I feel that every sufferer suffers in a different way. A lot has to be taken into consideration, but I personally feel the odds are in favour. I certainly thank God that I have been blessed with my daughter.

Margaret

A PERSONAL ACCOUNT

Following my medical diagnosis of chronic anxiety/depression, it was established that this condition was triggered through stress due to abnormal working hours and being a workaholic.

The first indication that something was wrong occurred when rising from bed to go to the toilet. My legs collapsed and I fell backwards into the bath.

At this stage, I went sick from work never to return, due to my progressive illness which slowly deteriorated when I was admitted into the first of my three attendances at a psychiatric hospital, having a total of 22 E.C.T. (electroconvulsive therapy) treatments. During the waiting time for the anaesthetist to apply the anaesthetic injection, I was in a terrible state of fear.

At one of my visits to see my doctor when, as always, I was accompanied by my wife (I could not attend or travel on my own) I was in such an anxious state that I moved all the items on my doctor's desk.

As I do not remember very much during my severe period of illness (total of 21 weeks in hospital) I have recently asked my wife how I behaved, and she gave the following account:

a) For long periods I used to lie in bed all day chanting continuously.

b) I paced up and down for hours on end.

c) I was convinced I would appear in the 'News of The World' as a malingerer.

d) I would hide behind buildings to avoid being seen by people I knew from work as I believed myself to be a malingerer.

e) I would hide underneath the driving wheel of my car when parked while waiting for my wife - reason as d) previous page.

Whilst I was suffering for four and a half years of illness, I can recall certain instances which stand out in my memory, although my memory power is still rather bad.

There was the occasion when I got out of bed during the night and went into my wife's bedroom and started to lean over her. She told me in the morning that she woke up terrified to see me standing over her with my depressed facial expression.

In another situation my wife was so upset seeing me in such a drugged state because of medication that she stopped giving me my prescription, and that was the start of approximately two weeks of sheer hell at night.

During this period, I experienced terrifying scenes in my head whilst hallucinating.

To get away from these scenes I tried to get out of my bedroom, but could not find the light switch or door.

When going through one of my worst spells, I tried to commit suicide by walking into a moving car, which braked and swerved fiercely to avoid me. On another occasion I took an overdose and was rushed to hospital.

During all this long period my wife stood by me. She used to visit me every day while I was in hospital, and gave me every kind of help and support possible at home. At the end of the four and a half years of caring and coping my wife has been diagnosed with angina, and I know my condition brought about this diagnosis.

It is now truly wonderful to feel so much better mentally that I am not worried by the physical conditions I have, such as: Murmuring heart (diagnosed 20 years ago).

1. Continuous tingling in my head which I have experienced for the past five years.

2. Worn disc at base of spine.
3. Cervical Spondylosis.
4. Tremulous Parkinsons.
5. Awaiting G.P. appointment for a further problem.

Anon

DEPRESSION - IDEAS AND THINGS TO DO WHEN FEELING LOW AND DEPRESSED

WRITTEN ON 15-9-94

Phone or tell someone (especially if very low).

Try to identify mood, i.e. fed up, depressed, suicidal, anxious, worried, annoyed (or don't know how you feel)

Things I could do - talk to someone,

go for a walk

Have a hot bath, wash hair,

play music/listen to radio,

watch T.V.

Avoid stressful situations and loud noise.

Try to be with other people.

If other people are annoying you, tell them.

Have some time to yourself if possible.

Do something nice for yourself or someone else.

Buy yourself a small treat or present - or do so for someone else.

Read a newspaper, good book or magazine.

Try to find the cause, or sit down with a piece of paper, do some doodling or write the problem/answer down.

If you are having problems making decisions, refer to work you have done on following page with the Doctor from the Lakes (September 94)

Write to someone if you want to.

Phone and go and see someone.

Don't let people treat you badly or upset you.

Talk to your child or children (if applicable). Phone them if they are away from home.

Talk to your partner/husband if you have one.

Don't make decisions if you feel unwell, or are not able to - it's better to decide something when you are feeling better and more sure of yourself. Struggling with a hard decision would be tough on yourself.

Give yourself a break, and don't feel guilty about it.

If someone offers some help or advice, take it if it feels right.

Don't do things you don't want - if you don't feel up to something, be kinder to yourself instead of punishing yourself.

Don't let people's advice confuse you - listen to it, then do what seems best for you. Don't feel guilty about what's happened because of your illness.

Try things but don't push yourself too hard, because things could go tumbling backwards!

Don't forget about your appearance - it's important for you to feel good about yourself, even if you are not going anywhere.

Think about your clothes, shoes, make-up, hair etc.

Try *not* to worry, sort problems out when you feel the time is right.

Think about *sleeping at night* - tomorrow will be a better day than today. But today is a good day anyway.

Think about flowers, birds, trees, the grass, animals, children etc.

THINGS TO AVOID

Having arguments with people - this brings you down, causes unsettlement.

Being too busy, having to be in too many different places at once adds to stress.

Don't have too many helpers or advisors, because you'll get confused - talk to the person who is helping you.

Sets of problems about those problems. The person who is helping you with something else about that, etc.

Seek out different people, places, don't plod along alone. That doesn't seem to get you anywhere.

Write down the problems - and what you would like to do about them.

When feeling depressed, do what has to be or is normally done that day.

Don't let depression take the whole day, or your whole life. Try and find some time or something to resolve it during the day.

IDEAS:

Keep a diary of thoughts and moods, especially if they are really changeable. Try to get other people to understand you and not criticize. You could even keep a chart of your moods.

Anon

The Doctor: The Lakes - Friday 23rd September 1994

1. Go out every day.
2. Meet people as much as possible.
3. Buy a newspaper every so often and read it.
4. Do things with your child (if applicable) or one you know. Go to the park, play with board games or toys, go for walks. Read him/her stories.
5. If facing difficult decisions, list the pros and cons, this will make it a lot easier.
6. If particularly low, contact G.P. on duty/doctor at the Lakes/ Peter.

7. Make own decisions and tell other people about those.
8. Tell people if unhappy about things.
9. Remember, better to do things than not.
10. If you are a parent, remind yourself that you are a good one, that you can look after your child very well.

Anon

A DIARY OF FEELING GOOD AND FEELING BAD

BY LINDA CUSICK

Introduction − I have been suffering mood swings since 1990. I have been in hospital a number of times and have had such vivid experiences with this illness that when I could I kept a diary to try and work out what was happening. Mostly I don't know whether to laugh or cry (actually I have done rather a lot of both!).

1.12.94
Just when things were beginning to settle, I started to get a bit overactive, with intense and exaggerated emotional outbursts which I couldn't control. I'm feeling things really strongly and I feel very excited. It's great to wake up and feel good instead of the usual dreadful feelings I get with depression.

I wonder how long this is going to last. My doctor tells me to be careful and think twice before I do anything but I am thinking about doing strange and dangerous things.

9.12.94
Still up and feeling pressurised, rushing a bit and only sleeping between 12.00 - 3.00 a.m. I'm taking medication to help.

2.1.95
My mood continued to go higher, and I did things which I thought weren't possible for me. I ended up having to go into hospital a few days before Christmas. Eventually, I calmed down.

20.1.95
The rushing thoughts and the feelings of totally delicious happi-

ness and laughing. I want to try and reduce all my drugs. I don't think I need them now; I can manage on my own.

2.2.95
I've had days and days of feeling really good, and thought it would last forever, but now it's all slipping away. I feel down, exhausted and depressed. I'm thinking bad thoughts.
I must get out of this.

9.3.95
I'm getting by at the moment, I'm not happy about gaining so much weight (three stones) since I have been taking the medication.

17.3.95
I'm feeling really bad again, so miserable, tearful, lacking the energy I had.

9.5.95
I just continue being depressed and feeling hopeless and not at all like communicating. But I am managing to get things done at work and at home now, though inside I feel empty and very unhappy.

31.5.95
I had about six weeks of depression and wondered if it was ever going to end, when suddenly I started to get fidgety and restless. Then I lost control and smashed a jam jar. After that, I wasn't able to concentrate or do much at all. I felt very uneasy, like I was being watched, that I might do anything, even dangerous things. I "saw" insects, animals, people, creeping into my side view, shouting in my head. I told myself off for being so stupid. It was so loud I had difficulty in stopping myself from throwing myself against the wall.

It faded slowly over the following two weeks, with a bit of help from the medication. I now feel calmer. If only I could stay like this (I've said this so many times before).

12.8.95

I dread doing things, they seem too much of an effort. I'm in a muddle, with a really strong sense of it all being unbearable, but when I push myself I do get some things done. It's all an effort though, almost torture. I never remember it being so difficult before. I'm still at the mercy of my moods. My peace of mind has gone again. And only a little while ago it came back and life seemed so easy.

31.10.95

Many weeks later and I have been in the longest depression I have had - 12 weeks. But now I'm gradually coming out of it. It feels a relief, although I still feel very bad in the mornings and don't have much energy or positivity.

19.1.96

My usual antidepressant seemed to take the edge off the depression. A couple of weeks later I started having difficulty sleeping, and then I got a bit high, so back on the tranquillisers. Then I experienced mixed moods, at times feeling very weepy and depressed and finding it difficult to do anything, then getting worked up and laughing a lot. This is really very difficult.

3.5.96

Still depressed and mentally and physically exhausted. It's been three months in this mood, and I can't help thinking it's not going to go. I know I must try and not think negatively, which is very hard.

End of May
Now I feel happier and more active although I've missed some days at work. I'm mostly brilliant at everything compared to how I just used to sit at my desk or in the armchair with my head down, struggling to work, taking ages over it. Now I can do it all and more besides, and it's no effort. I'm feeling more active, don't need much sleep, and have dreams and nightmares, which cause me to wake up confused. Wide awake at 4 a.m. It's all so funny when you think about it, how this all keeps happening to me.

26.10.96
A long time has gone by. I spent July to September quite depressed. The usual thing, I dreaded everything but then it went away.

25.4.97
Now I'm wondering what happened since November. I know I had a very bad patch. I was down for the rest of November and December. At the end of December, I got into an agitated state where I kept worrying about catastrophes that had not happened, but I believed they had. After the Christmas holiday I went back to my doctor and he gave me more appropriate medication. Since then, I'm getting short spells of depression, then some mood swings, feeling dreadful in the morning, followed by getting increasingly active and excited as the day goes on.

27.5.97
The days have gone by and they've brought many changes and anguish with only a little happiness. Sometimes I've lost my thoughts, sometimes my memory, sometimes I rage, sometimes laughing, shouting, and much pacing the house and garden.

4.7.97

I've been more depressed than for a long time. After a month on a new antidepressant I started to get agitated. The drugs didn't work. I got even more agitated, was prescribed haloperidol. I felt terrible, agitated and in a state of anxiety, I had to keep moving, pacing around and talking to cling on, just avoiding having to go into hospital. I felt unbearable panic and pressure. I also felt depressed. Then I started to get better, and since the middle of August I've been reasonably okay.

8.11.97

Despite getting a bit worked up and waking at 4-5 a.m. most nights, I'm getting by. This is the longest I have ever been okay for. Things are looking good now!

30.12.97

Things went badly wrong. I got more and more overactive, it was very enjoyable but almost out of control and if I'm honest I thought and did inappropriate things! In the end I couldn't control myself. My doctor said I was in a manic state, pacing about all over the place and laughing. He tried to persuade me to go into hospital immediately. I laughed. I thought he was joking, and said I could prove I was alright because I had it in writing, and showed him my notes. In the end, I agreed, because he said it was for the best, as if I continued as I was it would only be a matter of time before things got more out of hand. The police could get involved and it would turn nasty, and I could be in hospital for months or go into a very bad depression if we didn't control this high before it got even worse. So what could I do? I really wanted to go and do more shopping because that's what I had been doing that morning. I was really into shopping at this time, Christmas as well. Once in hospital I had to take the medicine and it literally knocked me out and worked on my mood and thoughts immediately. Then I realised the horror of my situation. It was awful in hospital, so terribly boring, terrible food. The smell and the side effects of the droperidol were horrendous; unbearable restlessness and agitation both mental and physical. I hardly saw my husband and the children and caused them all more worry, I couldn't believe how it had all happened.

28.1.98
I came out of hospital. By this time, I was beginning to feel depressed, dreading doing anything and feeling miserable. Doctor gave me a new antidepressant, which didn't work. I continued like this for four weeks, and then the depression got much worse. I could hardly do anything, couldn't go to work (I work part time in a school during term times) and things at home were very difficult. I spent all the morning and some of the afternoon in bed because I couldn't face things again. I was feeling frantic with the depression, it felt unbearable, and I didn't know how to stand it. I saw a doctor at an emergency appointment and asked if I could go back on my old antidepressant as it had helped me in the past, so I did and it took three weeks to work. Now it's 14.3.98 and I've been getting gradually better. Now I feel quite good.

7.5.98
I've been up and down so many times since I last wrote that I can't count them. Mostly though it's not been as severe as in the previous few months. Here's hoping for better times!

8.6.98
This is the longest time I've been okay (how many times have I got to this and then it all goes wrong for me). But now I really do feel my normal self, in fact it feels a bit boring! Some people are never satisfied!

DEAR DIARY

Went on leave from hospital Saturday to Sunday. I felt like I did before I came in the hospital. I was trying to cook dinner and it all felt like an effort.

I just sat there. I didn't feel like doing anything, but felt awful for not doing anything. There were times that I enjoyed, like watching the telly in the evening, eating jacket potato and prawns and helping my husband with the crossword.

When I got back to hospital on Sunday, I was upset. I cried because I felt no better than I had when I came in to the hospital.

Monday I cried because I thought of all these things I have written. Of knowing how I feel.

Wednesday and Thursday felt really good.

I feel as if I don't want the hum-drum life at home. It just seems to depress me.

What is wrong with me? Is it manic or is it just me?

Margaret

The artist was putting across feelings of confusion and
utter despair, with a mind feeling muddled and
expressing tears of emotion.

THREE YEARS ILLNESS

One of my first bad experiences that led from my illness was when I first became ill.

I thought I had a terminal illness. I think that was a way of escaping. I didn't understand why I was so unhappy, why I had no will to live, why I enjoyed being drunk so much, not socializing, crying continuously, blackouts. The list goes on.

So as I was 15 and missing school my mother took me to the doctor, who didn't consider what I said, and didn't listen. He just prescribed my mother antidepressants to cope with me.

If the doctor had paid more attention I wouldn't have had to go to the 13 - 16 year olds' Psychiatric Unit, and spend the next three years trying to become a normal teenager again. How I would love to worry about the things girls my age usually fuss about. After feeling like a shadow with no future or possibilities in life for years, it's hard to understand, now I'm better, what to do or think. Now I'm expected to throw myself straight in the deep end, which is very hard after being in such isolation.

I'm now doing a Princes Trust Volunteer's Course that I would recommend to anyone who has recovered after problems.

I'm just worried what I'm supposed to do once the course has finished.

I think that the Doctors should have someone that they can send people like me to, even if it is only slight symptoms. It would save a lot of time, pain and money.

Jennifer, age 18

MANIC

This piece was written when I was in the grip of Manic Depression. I think I must have been feeling high.

When you're in hospital, they make you sleep. When you wake, you eat, sleep, and receive therapy. It's great fun, you get three meals provided and you can be as silly as you like while you're in there. You can have a second childhood! After all, they expect it of you, and you wouldn't want to disappoint them would you?

Leading up to your admission, you become really interested in what you have become involved with. So you become more active as you are enjoying it, more confident. I was once taught assertiveness skills, which these days have proved very useful. (But at that time, because I did change, people did not respond well. I had changed, I was keeping busy. "Crumbs, watch out, she'll be back in that hospital acting like this!") So everything I do is scrutinized. It becomes annoying, I am not a child. All those closest to you become angered and authoritative. The ones you need most for support can't cope, yet it is me who ends up in hospital. When you need those closest to you, to be there for you, they turn against you, you are alone. Still, at least you have three free meals provided, and have your washing done for you by your 'caring' relations.

Nobody ever seems to be able to find out what is the root of the problem.

They never take that much notice of what you tell them. It is really odd. If you have a broken leg, there is an awful amount of fuss made. X-rays, location of pain, nice nurse popping in regularly to tuck you in. It's not like that for people like me. I remember once they asked what I did, and so I told them that I was a brain surgeon.

They hardly spent any time with you, though one nurse did, but she was having a break from working and having a cigarette, which I believe she should not have done. They take breaks from work to sit with the patient, so she gets back to doing her paperwork, such is the life of a caring, sharing psychiatric nurse. At least if she gave stamps it would be a beneficial process.

Anon

93-94 (21.7.96)

FED UP OR DEPRESSED?

Have you ever been told to "pull yourself together"? Have a good clean up in the kitchen, make loads of cakes? Does it really help someone suffering depression? These are some of the things I've been advised to do in the past. Most people's understanding of depression tends to be that someone is very fed up. They don't understand what suffering depression is really like.

In my experience, I have found that no matter what I do, nothing helps. You can clean out the whole house, make thousands of cakes, but it makes no difference. That is the difference between being fed up and being depressed. With feeling fed up you can do something and it lifts you out of it. With depression, no matter what you do, you still feel the same, and that's what is so hard to live with. How do you feel when you are stuck in a traffic jam, on a hot day, with no chance of it clearing for hours? At least you know that a time will come that you will arrive at your destination. But with depression, it is like being in a traffic jam for months on end. I myself have suffered from manic depression. This form of depression means that the sufferer has a 'high' and then has a 'low'. I have found that I become very happy, and feel a need to do all the things I have wanted to do, like cleaning the house, visiting all my friends, finishing making that dress, cook all those cakes for the freezer, tidy up the garden, you name it, I had to do it, and would be so enthusiastic, there was no time to waste. On the go, all the time. Until, eventually family and friends would become very worried about me, and, not knowing how to deal with it, would often come across as being hostile, which would seem to me as though they hated me and were trying to get rid of me. So, in the end, the only safe haven would be hospital. I would then come down to earth - so to speak - and gradually feel well and then go home. Once home, I would be well for a while, and then find myself feeling depressed. While being in an in between state, I would be very wary of doing too much and ending up 'high' again, so being cautious meant life became dull, which led to feeling depressed, which meant living a very unhappy life. All I wanted to do was sit around, watching the clock, not wanting time to pass, because I knew time was passing, time which I knew I was wasting, but could do nothing about. It was no good talking to friends and relations, they didn't understand. If it wasn't for the Dove Centre (a mental health centre) and the Baddow Day Unit (a day centre linked to the hospital) and seeing the Doctor connected to the hospital, and the Samaritans, how would I have coped? Relations were too close and couldn't help because they didn't know how, which led to them ending up frustrated, angry and upset. Friends, except those who I met through my illness, couldn't help, and their advice would simply annoy me due to their lack of understanding of what I was going through. At the beginning of my struggle with this illness I would turn to friends, but it would only make matters worse, and I later found it was best not to let friends and relations know if I wasn't feeling too good and they were better as friends when they were unaware of my predicament.

Margaret

The Dove Centre and Baddow Day Unit are no longer in Chelmsford

KNOWING THE SIGNS

When I was first ill and experiencing a 'high' it was impossible to appreciate that the way I was behaving was because of an illness. Due to the fact that there was quite a gap of time between each bout of illness, I would find that when I was well, I would have settled into the security of being well and I would feel that that was the norm. It was hard for me to appreciate I was ill. I feel these days I am much more aware of the fact that I do suffer from this illness, and appreciate and take heed of what my husband is saying when he is trying to warn me that I am acting in a way that makes alarm bells ring for him. I am very lucky to have a husband who has stuck by me over the years. He is the one who knows me better than anyone. He cares and he has come to know the danger signs. I know that if someone like me is experiencing lack of sleep or appetite it is time to take note. So when my husband starts to become concerned, I know I must take his opinion very seriously. We have a very good relationship, and so when our relationship begins to feel strained, I am learning to take note. Another sign that I am becoming ill is when I start continuously listening to and watching Cliff Richard. I know that some people would agree that too much of Cliff Richard would have a serious effect on anyone! I do get teased! On a more serious note, I guess I just reach a stage due to my illness that I need a bit of escapism. I just go into my own world where I am right and people can't reason with me. I'm just not me anymore. We know it is time to seek professional help, so it's off to hospital for me. Sometimes when things are going really well for me, maybe too well and I am feeling 'high', I go to bed and lay there awake for quite a while, but I have learnt that I mustn't get up out of bed, no matter how restless I feel. The danger would be if I did get up, as I have in the past, and find myself ending up hardly getting any sleep, I would just be making drinks all night. I know if I stay in bed I will eventually get off to sleep.

As I mentioned earlier, lack of appetite is also a bad sign. This has never really affected me, as I love my food, and if anything I eat more when I am going through a bad patch as this is the only thing that I get any sort of pleasure from.

Margaret

HOW IT USED TO FEEL AND HOW DO I COPE?

How It Used to Feel When I Was Ill

How can I describe how I feel when I am really ill? I guess there is just a lack of interest in anything I do. All I feel I have to look forward to is the effort of getting up in the morning, the effort of eating my breakfast, it is all an effort. Nothing is of interest to me, so all I have to look forward to is the effort of living. If I don't do the washing, how do I get anything clean to wear? How can I not iron things? It would be far worse to go around wearing something that hasn't been ironed. I have a husband and daughter and I used to feel that I needed to do all the housework. I felt it was my job, even though I felt bad. Nothing makes you feel better, so all I do is cry - sometimes when I'm really ill even crying doesn't help.

So what can you do? All you're left with is a constant struggle and a constant barrage of things you *must* do. No, having a nice hot bath is of no consolation, it's just another struggle, another necessity that has to be done. So what if I do nothing? That is even more frustrating - having nothing to do, just endless time with nagging reminders that I *have* to do things. If I'm lucky, I find crying helps, it soothes away the pent-up feelings of frustration and despair.

How Life Is for Me Today? (January 1998)

Yes, I have a husband and daughter who try to help me when I'm ill, they comfort me. I used to feel that I should be the one who struggles with all the housework and things that need doing (it was my job). I used to think it was the only way to beat this illness. I was sure that keeping up with everything was the only way to cope. Then in 1996 I was ill in hospital, and it was suggested that I joined the 'Solutions Focus' group at the Linden Centre, which I did when I later became a day patient. It has helped me immensely. Each week, we met with two members of staff who led the group. We wrote down the things that have happened during the week and the staff helped us to see the positive things in what we had written. I have learnt through this group and the people of The Rainbow Clubhouse' about how others cope when they are going through a tough time. I have learnt that life with mental illness does not have to be as difficult as I was making it for myself. I have learnt to assess how much I can cope with and how much I need my family to help me. A friend at The Rainbow Clubhouse said that I needed to ask myself what was more important, the housework or myself? From Solution Focus I have learnt about the ways that other people in the group are coping with the illness. I used to have a very strict routine of housework, but I am learning now about being flexible. I find I do not have to do my ironing religiously on a Monday (which is how I am happy to do things when I am well). If I am not feeling up to it I can do it over the next few days, a little at a time. I can clean the bathroom on a Saturday if I feel like it, instead of dreading doing it the following week. If I am feeling really bad, I hope to be able to just forget housework. I did, once. I had a break from it for a few days when I felt I *should* have been doing it.

I found when I was better I felt in the mood to do it.

Margaret

The Rainbow Clubhouse has since closed.

WOULD I WISH THIS ON MY WORST ENEMY?

When people experience an awful illness they often say they wouldn't wish anyone else to experience what they are going through. I don't know if I could be that charitable.

With the majority of illnesses that people experience, others can appreciate how much they are suffering because everyone knows what physical pain is like. With mental illness, only a sufferer can appreciate the hell that people experience. It is not seen and the nearest most people come to suffering mental illness is, like the tip of the iceberg, when they find themselves really fed up. So as far as I'm concerned, I sometimes feel a kind of relief if I hear someone has experienced what mental illness is all about for themselves. It is then that I feel I have another soul mate who I can relate to. I usually find myself feeling this way when I am ill and in need of some understanding. When I am well, I then feel that I really wouldn't wish it on anyone else.

Margaret

A REASON

Mother died last Wednesday:
(at least you've got a reason)
Horse ran his last race.
(at least you've got a reason)
Forgot to buy my lottery ticket - I would have won.
(well at least you've got a reason)
What's your game?
    Why sit and mope?
        You've got no reason.
A home, a car, a husband, a this, a that.
    I KNOW!
Why do I feel so depressed?
    I have no reason.
        Guilty I am made to feel.
            Suicide looks good to me.
Still no reason, still to blame.
    It's my fault, I guess.
        Just leave me alone.

                        Margaret

<u>GONE</u>

Gone

Black tears
Softly dropped
Dripped
Whispers
Kissed your lips
Fingertips But

You did not feel
You did not see
You did not hear
Dead to me.

Audra Gardner 1998

SOLITUDE

EMPTY NOTHINGNESS

I feel full of empty nothingness
I turn to you, my nearest and dearest
   and still there's empty nothingness.
We cuddle
   and all I feel is empty nothingness.
I've tried a lie in bed, a handful of chocolate treats
   but all there is is an empty nothingness.
I cry, as I have cried so many times
   and with time,
      A day comes when my tears
        help soothe the pain.
Empty nothingness is what I fear.
It is always there
   when I'm in the grips of despair.
Nothing but days to dread
   and nights to dread the day which threatens:
      my daunting tomorrows.

                         Margaret

<u>EXHAUSTING</u>

Exhausted, I'm so exhausted.
Do this, do that, I'm the boss,
   And boss I do, I can't stop,
      Oh, I wish I could just drop!
Right now I'm feeling high
   Can I reach the sky?
I would be able to only yesterday,
   But now, I just give myself orders.
Would it feel beautiful if I had a rest?
   Inside am I doing it all for the best?
It's beyond my jurisdiction
   to stop and display common
      sense in a common sense sort of way.
Where is all my energy?
   All gone, it has been spent.
And yes I'd hate to be bored
   For that can only mean
      depression is back taking a hold
And down that road
   I don't think I'm ready to be sold.

                          Margaret

TURN OFF THE ON SWITCH

Oh please turn off the on switch
I keep doing this and doing that.
    Don't I ever stop?
I'm in remote control
I can't stand a dull moment
    Every minute's got to be filled with excitement
        of adventure of gain
I grasp the next inspiration
When one is hard to find
    I'm in despair
        I'm in a whirl, I'm grasping at straws
I need a break
An hour or so of rest
    But no, I must continue
        My desperate quest
It's all too much
    My feelings of exhaustion
        Finally come to a head
I drop on the settee
    And I'm out like a light.
I wake, and peace and harmony reign
    Until the next
        Dull moment grips my being
        And I'm off again.

Margaret

When I am well I feel warm like the sun shining on a summer's day. Free and easy with not a care in the world. When I am ill I feel down and murky, like a puddle with no escape.

HIGHS' AND 'LOWS'

I suffer from manic depression. People who suffer from manic depression experience 'highs' and 'lows'. When I get high I have an abundance of energy. There are not enough hours in the day to do all the things I want to do; I just want to do everything. My husband becomes very concerned and very worried. I can only interpret this as him becoming annoyed with me, as though he only wants to spoil my fun. When eventually I do calm down, which is usually in hospital, I then discover what the 'lows' are all about. It's hard to explain to people what the lows are about. I find when I am experiencing them they really are awful. Some people may advise me to do something like bake lots of cakes to make me feel better, but nothing makes you feel better. It's not something you can get out of. It wouldn't be so bad if you knew that from 6 p.m. to 10 p.m. life would be wonderful, and the rest would be hell, you could then at least have a few hours when it would all be O.K., but it doesn't work like that, it's with you all the time.

Margaret

I enjoy writing poetry. Here are two which, for me, sum up some of the unpleasant feelings that accompany mental illness.

NEGATIVE FEELINGS

Negative feelings like great black vultures hover above me.
Flapping wings blot out the sun,
Raucous screeching drowns all other sound.
Positive feelings are only a thought away.

Negative feelings like dark storm clouds gather round me.
Their density blots out the sun,
Rumbling thunder drowns all other sounds.
Positive feelings are only a thought away.

Positive feelings - so near - yet so far.
Reach through the gloom as to a distant star,
Clasp that happy thought, clutch that ray of hope.
Positive feelings - so near - yet so far.

Negative feelings heavy and foreboding
slowly, yet surely, grinding, crushing, weighing me down.
Positive feelings are only a thought away.
Could I but grasp that thought!

Jenny Porteous

ISOLATION

Sometimes I feel like screaming.
So many thoughts and feelings lie hidden,
Just below the surface of my mind.
Dark brooding bitter memories,
yet, when spoken, sounding so feeble,
almost laughable - except there is nothing to laugh at.
And if I try to put them into words they disappear.
Back into my mind, back into the depth of my soul,
to wait until I am alone,
till night-time comes and sleep eludes me.
Then they re-appear.
Rising again to haunt me with their mocking,
Until I cry 'why won't you set me free'.
Sometimes, very often, I feel like screaming, screaming,
screaming, SCREAMING.
But who the hell will hear me if I do?

Jenny Porteous

I CAN'T DO ANYTHING RIGHT

I can't do anything right,
    It feels as if all we ever do is fight.
When I am high
    You quickly fly
        Into a rage
Things can't really be this bad!
    It leaves me feeling really sad.
I guess because you care
    My 'high' behaviour leads you to despair
I get upset
    It's beyond my control
        I'm really sorry if I drive you up the pole.
Tomorrow the future may look a lot brighter
    I always feel in me there's one hell of a fighter.

Margaret

WAR ZONE

It's a war zone.
No peace can be found
    There's madness all around.
Husband and daughter
    Not acting as I think they ought'a.
How can they be flesh and blood?
    I don't want to be brought down with a thud.
Life is too much fun.
They're watching me run
    After every whim,
        They don't like the din.
Common sense prevails
    I add up all the sums
        And I feel I can't be right.
Yes, maybe I'm ill
    Am I acting against my will?
A few months in hospital and I'll be well on the way
    To find this darkness is replaced by a bright sunny day.

Margaret

I SHOULD BE SO LUCKY!

You may feel that as I suffer from manic depression, I should be cursing God for making me suffer like I do. But I find I can appreciate so much from the fact that I am a sufferer. Although I experience some of the worst feelings possible, I find that in my experience I can see some benefits of this disposition. I have family who stand by me even though they experience their own kind of hell. They could easily walk away and have nothing to do with me, but they don't. They cope with it all as best as they can - and I must say they have learnt over the years to cope really well. Friends and I have grown together and I know exactly how genuine they are. I have also made friends with others who have suffered like me, who are wonderful, as they know exactly how awful this illness is, and although they suffer as well, we are strong for each other. As family and friends, we have a deep understanding and love for one another. I know what people have gone through for me, and I can only marvel at it. I am truly lucky.

I am fortunate to live in an area where there is an abundance of people who work within mental health. There are C.P.N.s (Community Psychiatric Nurses), as well as the Rainbow Clubhouse, The Dove Centre, The Mill, The Linden Centre and the Samaritans, all within the Chelmsford area.

I am extremely humble, through this book, to read other people's accounts of their experiences of life with me, Margaret Mitchell. Some people may go through life without experiencing any kind of trauma. Life must seem very mundane and uninteresting. For me, I find when I am well I have a lot of people to thank and marvel at their care and steadfastness. I have a lot to thank God for.

Margaret

The Rainbow Clubhouse and the The Dove Cente are no longer in Chelmsford.

MALE THINKING

I sometimes hate being a man;
Finding it hard to be,
Sensitive and emotional;
But feeling I should keep it inside.

I feel stronger,
With so much emotion
Bubbling inside my soul.

But sometimes I feel
It's not normal,
To have such feelings;
And guilt and shame,
Raise their heads again.

So quickly I raise the barriers,
And pretend that they're not there.
And then I do something stupid...

And then I act like a man.

STEVE

PARTY TIME

Here I am
   So alone.
I fight my way through the crowds of people
   To find a singular iced bun
     Just sitting there, on its own.
Tears well up inside as a haze of faces
   Join in social intercourse.
This is no place for me to be
   I just can't stand the pain.
I can't stand the intermit closeness
   That exists for everyone else but me.
This lonesome heart that I bear
   Can not be reached.
The distance I feel between myself and the world
   Is planets apart.
What can I do?
   I must soldier on and just be patient.
Another day for me to face,
   These feelings of being lost
     Amongst another crowd, for yet another day.

Margaret

When you have problems you feel you are the only one, and lonely even though there is family around.

SOLITAIRE

Empty and frustrated
        is often how I feel.
Surely there's no way to escape!
Only tears to shed
        and fears to dread.
This life I must cope with on my own.
For it's a sufferer only who can share
        these thoughts that destroy the life I bear.
Help me please, is often what I plead.
        I'm someone who is in desperate need.
Will a tomorrow ever I see?
Are peace and contentment for the likes of me?
How can I be sure they'll be a future bright?
        that will be worth living, a pure delight?

Margaret

ALLISON HARTNEY HELP LINE
JOHN HAYES BBC ESSEX TUESDAY 18TH MAY 1993 9.35 A.M.
MALDON MIND NETWORK

My first major attack of mental illness came after a major operation 26 years ago.

I became deeply depressed and had to have shock treatment. When we moved house I became very lonely and suffered a complete breakdown. I have had operations and suffered mental illness ever since.

Mental illness cannot be seen, so people do not understand how ill you feel. It's a very lonely feeling.

Getting out to MIND Group once a week has helped me a lot. I can talk to people about my illness and do not feel alone with it.

Jean Lomas

SUFFERING

I think it is a natural law
And it is my firm belief
That the greater the suffering
The greater the joy of relief.

Though suffering can seem eternal
With no end in sight,
It may seem like a battle,
A never ending fight.

Usually relief is gradual
And doesn't often come over night,
But it can come suddenly
Like an eagle in flight.

It is also a fact of life
Many people suffer the most
Just prior to meeting
the heavenly host.

This law is true for everyone
No matter what you believe
For even annihilation
Is a form of reprieve.

So suffering exists
For us to overcome
And I believe this will be achieved
In the third millennium!

Jim Wilson

SUFFERING 2

I think it is a natural law
And it is my firm belief,
That the greater the suffering
The greater the joy of relief.

However, it is crucial
That a person has insight
Into their suffering
And unfortunate plight.

For there are people who may appear
To be in a predicament
But, in themselves
They are quite happy and content.

Then suffering brought on
By a person's own brewing,
Holds no sympathy
It's uncertain and unclear.

Then when relief comes
It will be so great,
Like the lifting
Of a leaden weight.

It will seem like a new lease
Of good fortune,

Like a butterfly emerging
From a cocoon.

Like passing on through
A heavenly door
Into an existence
That could last forever more!

Jim Wilson

CRYING

Here I go again, crying, why *do* I cry? People say "Oh, don't cry", but why shouldn't I? "Pull yourself together then," someone replied. I am not a pair of curtains! When I get this frustrating, tense feeling inside, the best way of dealing with it is to cry. What is so wrong with crying? If God didn't give us tears for shedding, then why do we have them? A good cry is the best medicine for me to use when I feel I need to release my pent-up feelings.

Some may shed their pent-up feelings by kicking down a brick wall, what would you prefer?

I am fortunate enough to have places to go to like The Rainbow Clubhouse. It is especially for people like me who suffer with mental illnesses. I find I can feel myself while I'm there and cry if I feel the need. The staff and members are very understanding, and if a good cry is needed I feel at home to do just that. I guess everyone there deals with their feelings in their own way. I don't often see others crying, just now and again, but with me I go for periods when that is all I feel I need to do. If it works for me then who has the right to take that away from me? When I do feel better and the sun is shining for me once again, I feel I can get a lot out of life, which is when I have to be careful I don't do too much. Crying for me is like a safety valve. The relief I feel after a good cry is immeasurable. It doesn't always solve the whole problem, but it certainly helps.

Margaret

HEADACHE

Most people can appreciate what the pain of a headache is like. No one can see a headache, only the sufferer can appreciate how awful it is. Just imagine if there were no effective fast working drugs and the pain went on for months. That is what a mentally ill person has to put up with. Mental illness is similar, with a mental pain that continues on and off for months at a time. It is unbearable to live with that pain. The pain is of a different nature to a headache, but most people can appreciate what a miserable existence that would be. It is very difficult to get any satisfaction out of anything. I suppose, the thing is if you suffer with a headache you know what the problem is and it will go away, but with depression the medication you take could take up to six months, even a year to be effective, so nothing can be done and you are left to suffer for that amount of time.

Margaret

ANTICIPATION

I find when I am suffering from manic depression, I can tell a few minutes after I've woken up in the morning just how I'm going to feel that day. If all is well I wake up feeling relaxed and at one with the world, but if I wake up feeling all panicky and worried I know straight away that I am in for a difficult time. As I have suffered with this illness for many years, I know all the signs, and if I am feeling at my worst in the morning when I wake up, that is the hardest time. With this illness I find the evening is my best time, but having said that it is spoilt as I have my worst time - in the morning - to anticipate and dread. So I can never win. When I reach a 'good' time within my day, I am left only to dread at that time what I will have to endure in the near future.

Margaret

HEAVY WEIGHTS

With mental illness it feels as if you have some weights pulling you down. If you were a body builder and you picked up some very heavy weights, the strain would grow as you picked them up. You would be able to lift them up above your head and hold them there until the strain became unbearable, then you would have to drop them back down on to the floor. Mental illness feels as though you have heavy weights pulling you down. The mental pain is very similar, but you cannot drop the weight of pain, it just goes on hurting.

Margaret

DECISIONS

I find when I am not well, decisions are very hard to make. I lose all my confidence and end up in a real state of panic and anxiety. Even things like knowing how much washing I can put in the washing machine, things I've done countless times, seem to be impossible decisions to make. I have to keep asking obvious questions. It can be very difficult. Through my experiences, I have learnt to take my time and slowly measure up my options.

Margaret

A.W.O.L.

This was the beginning of recognising through therapy the needs I had as a child, and often as an adult, that were never met - why I'd always felt different from other children and, later, adults. These things were absent in my life and I was beginning, with my therapist help, to understand this and to learn to try and replace some of these needs myself. A.W.O.L. was literally things in my life that were 'Absent Without Leave' without my permission. I had no control or power, especially as a child, to change this.

A.W.O.L.

There's a bit of me that's missing,
I'm complete but never whole
I can see I have a body
But it doesn't fit my soul

Like a jigsaw that's been started
But then is left undone
Or a story that has finished
Before it has begun.

I'm a church without a steeple
With a priest that has no prayer
In this world with many people
Without hope but much despair.

I'm the hand that cannot grip
I'm the mouth that cannot eat
I'm a dislocated hip
I'm a heart without a beat.

I'm the wind without a breeze
I'm a stream that doesn't flow
I'm a forest with no trees
I'm the plant that didn't grow.

I'm a bird within a cage
That was never free to fly
I'm the anger without rage
I'm the tears that couldn't cry.

I'm the nightmare, not the dream
Not in heaven but in hell
I'm the voice that cannot scream
I'm the child that couldn't tell.

17th May 1997   Jacqueline Monger

DREAD

This is something I suffer with when I am experiencing anxiety. I find I dread all things such as having a bath, cooking the meal, doing the housework, phoning people, more or less everything. I even dread having to go out in the evening, as the only thing I enjoy is watching the television at home, but then I dread time passing and the evening ending - I find I just can't win!

Margaret

PANIC

I stopped writing because my hand was shaking. I half expected the words to twist about, to unravel themselves before my eyes. Looking around the room, my eyes alighted on a large red book as red as blood. The photographs on the bookshelves seemed to look at me with glittering eyes, and the colour of everything seemed heightened, but outside all was sombre green. I stared at the large crack in the ceiling and somehow that was calming gradually. I began to feel more relaxed, closed my eyes, and, putting my head down on the table, I was conscious of the sunlight drifting through the window. I drifted into a daze.

Anon

THE NIGHTMARE

The nightmare has only just begun
Why am I constantly on the run?
How do I define my sanity?
Madness intertwined with profanity.
Friends and family long gone from this earth.
Was my mind corrupted from birth?
The extent of my plight is about to begin
Is this retribution for all the times I have sinned?
Do I deserve this punishment bestowed upon me?
I tend to think not, who on this planet holds the key?
The very key to life as we know it
But reality seems reluctant to show it.
So many answers yet to be revealed
The secrets of my life are carefully concealed.
Six months of my life in an institution
Is this really retribution?
How do I escape my maniacal conscience?
Only to live life on a whim of grim chance.
The walls come tumbling down
Confusion all around
It's time to take a stance and hold my ground
And leave this place to go homeward bound.
Should I return I hope to defer?
To live my life, I shall conquer.

Andrew C

MY PERSONAL EXPERIENCE OF ANXIETY

This is a condition I have suffered from. It is a most unpleasant experience. I feel it is in many ways worse than depression. When I have felt anxious I would feel things must go according to my plans. If something came up and I had to change my plans, I would find it unbearable. I would feel panicky and in a desperate state of turmoil. I just wouldn't be able to cope with it. I would hyperventilate, cry, pace, maybe even scream and bang my fists in despair. I felt I had to keep to my planned routine and it would take me a while to calm down as I would desperately try to adapt my routine to this new obstacle.

Margaret

THE DUST MONSTER

Housework, housework, won't it ever let me be?
  Will the big Dust Monster come and get me?
I am a prisoner locked in a cell.
  I hold the key,
    I must release me.
      From all this toil and trouble.
Surely I am the boss,
  Oh go and leave me be, I'm at a loss.
I'll spray you with my polish,
  But that's what you want, for me to demolish.
I must learn to ignore you
  For a while, leave me be
I'm hoping depression won't swallow up me.
The Dust Monster keeps on haunting,
  Won't it ever go and stop taunting?

Margaret

<u>NORMAL</u>

<u>(Dedicated to a friend)</u>

What is normal?
Tell me, you seem to know.
Why don't you leave me be?
To roam, to sing, to go
    Here and there,
I'm a free spirit.
Don't lock me away.
Who are you to judge me?
I'm in control.
You have no right.
Why not leave me be?
Can't I be the one to judge?
Why can't I be right?

Margaret

NORMAL

I do have long periods when I do feel 'normal'. To begin with, when I start to feel normal I really marvel at how wonderful it feels. Waking up in the morning and needing time to come to, but feeling contented. Getting up is no hardship and eating breakfast is a pleasurable experience, feeling relaxed and hungry. I take the day in my stride just feeling I can cope with whatever the day brings. Being able to juggle things about to fit in all my plans for the day. If I was ill all this would be a nightmare. I would wake up, wide awake, dreading having to get up, have breakfast and dread the day that faces me. I would have planned out the day and every day a while back as everything must neatly fit in to each day. Any change of routine would be a nightmare and almost impossible to cope with. For example, having a bath must strictly be in my routine, every Monday and Thursday - it couldn't be altered (I must add that I have a bath more frequently and on different days now I am well). What was most important was watching the television in the evenings. It would be impossible for me to cope without having my days focused around watching the television in the evenings. I found life was a little more tolerable as long as I was allowed to be left in peace to watch T.V. in the evening. I would find it unbearable if someone phoned for me during the evening, which I hated my-self for as I feel people come before the television, so feeling this way went against everything I believed in.

I guess I just have to be grateful that these periods of illness in my life do not go on for ever, and I must thank friends and family for their understanding and support during these difficult periods in my life.

Margaret

THE COAT

Why do I march with this coat on my back
when I can see the sunshine?
It's rough and heavy, but safe, protective.
What price is security?
Too comfortable to change.
But now I feel discomfort
What would I risk to remove it?
Vulnerability.
How bad is that?
I do want to change my code of dress
but its weight reminds me
of all that I have come to rely on,
to need, to live.
Without it what is left?
Only me, and what is that?
This coat is me and I am it
My Entity.
I want to remove it, see what results.
Perhaps not.
I will take it off, but carry it, by my side
Close enough to still be a part of me
And let exposure reveal the soul beneath
But the temptation to redress
Is too threatening, too close.
I don't want to compromise,
I want to be free, truly free.
I'll take it off and give it away, throw it away.

It's not mine anymore.
Out of date, inappropriate
Why do I let it fashion my life?
Still it seems to fit
Whatever shape, size, mood - it covers all.
Like a veil, a shroud,
a coat of arms.

Anon

I wrote this about two months after being admitted to Hospital when I felt sometimes people didn't know how to respond to me, or what to say or maybe just felt uncomfortable dealing with abuse. It was to say, "it's not always clever words I need, sometimes I just need a hug." The child inside me needed to be hugged, and I wasn't able to do that for myself as I'd never received hugs as a child. After a while I was referred to a therapist who was able to understand me and began to teach me to do this for myself. I knew then that given time, she was the person I really felt I could get better with.

IS ANYBODY THERE?

A hug is all I need sometimes
But no-one's ever there;
Do I really matter?
Does anybody care?

Am I so disgusting?
Am I really bad?
Enough to make you go away
And leave me feeling sad?

I bare my soul on paper,
I write my thoughts in ink,
I hide them all away because
I know what people think.

Do you find it difficult
Knowing what to say?
Would it just be better
If I put it all away?

I don't expect a miracle
But just to know you care;
A hug is all you need sometimes,
Is anybody there?

2nd October 1996   Jacqueline Monger

HOW IT IS

When I am feeling well it makes me really appreciate how lucky I am to be alive! Everything is wonderful. I get up in the morning feeling relaxed and at one with the world. I have my own home and a wonderful husband and daughter. There are clothes in the wardrobe, and food in the house, also a radio, a television and my own choice of music albums and videos. I feel relaxed and have the freedom to walk or travel anywhere I want to go. Living in England to me is a privilege; we're not rich and not poor. When I am ill, life is very different, and I can't enjoy the privileges of these things. Life just seems an effort, and when I wake up in the morning I cannot appreciate anything, it all seems just an effort and things feel like chores. Everything is a burden and small problems seem like major difficulties. I cannot relax and am anxious all the time. I make myself follow a tight schedule and know that I'd feel ten times worse if I didn't get things done. All the time there are decisions to make which rush at me from all angles, my memory doesn't work as well and so I usually leave written messages here and there for myself as reminders. Life is just impossible, what can I do but carry on? It is so hard to appreciate the fact that this difficult life of mine will not always be this way. I need constant reminders of the fact that all this suffering will one day come to an end and I will be well again.

So when the day does come, I am able to appreciate how fortunate I am and how beautiful life can be, thank God.

Margaret

HOW DOES IT FEEL?

When I am going through a rough patch, it just seems to go on for ever. I just feel awful, and I can't see an end to it. I find that if I can cry it helps a lot. It is as if I have pent up frustration inside me and crying is a form of release. I remember once when I was ill and I just couldn't cry, it was awful. I find when I'm feeling ill, the best way to cope is to keep on going, keep on doing the housework, cooking the meals, attend the Day Hospital and The Rainbow Clubhouse of which I am a member. I know that if I stay in bed or neglect my housework, I will feel worse. At least if I carry on doing things there is a sense of accomplishment. It's hard to sum up exactly how it feels. Imagine that you have badly crashed your new beautiful car; how would you feel? That's the kind of feeling you get: but it doesn't go away, it's there twenty-four hours a day.

Margaret

The Rainbow Clubhouse has since closed.

SELF EXPRESSION

I have found that self-expression
Helps to defeat depression
So if your life is full of sorrow
And you can hardly bear to face tomorrow
Try to set aside a little time today
To express yourself in a positive way
Even if you live on your own
Try speaking to someone on the phone
Or by writing someone a letter
You will feel a whole lot better
Please believe me because I know
After years of feeling constantly low
By expressing myself, I've managed to survive
And now at times, I feel glad, to be alive!

Jim Wilson

CAN'T BE VERY BRIGHT THEN?

I sometimes think that people may feel that if you suffer from mental illness you lack intellect. I guess I feel it must look like that if someone is mentally weak, but this can't be the case when you put together talented people like Spike Milligan, Vincent Van Gogh, Tony Hancock, Paul Merton, Nicola Paget and Terry Thomas.

Surely it must make you think twice. I think people who suffer often strive for perfection and give their all, and if they can't find perfection, there is nothing left but to fall on imperfection, and that is just unacceptable to them.

Through my illness I have come across some very talented people who are extremely gifted. I have seen many high quality works of art, and some that are destroyed by their maker due to the imperfection that that person feels is unacceptable.

We do not live in a perfect world, most of us can accept that and live a happy life, but to some people it is something that, through illness, can seem unacceptable.

Margaret

MY HUSBAND AND I

I will have been married for 20 years in September. For any marriage to run smoothly for that length of time would be most unusual. For a marriage to survive 20 years and to have coped with the added pressure of mental illness is something to be proud of, and proud of it I am. My husband has stuck by me through thick and thin since my illness began, 18 years ago now, when I experienced post-natal depression after having our daughter, Michelle. I know how strong our marriage is, as we have had to endure very long periods of the manic depression from which I suffer. By reading this book, you will be able to appreciate just how patient my husband, Stewart, has been. As a couple we have managed to survive years of turbulence. I know that if my husband can stick by me through everything we have experienced in the past, then we can survive anything.

When I am well, and there have been quite long periods when I have been well, we very much enjoy our time together. When I am ill, things like decorating, or plans for doing something major in our garden just don't get done. So it feels very exciting when I am well, for us to plan something major and succeed in completing the task in hand. We can plan outings or go to the theatre or on excursions. These are things which everyone takes for granted, but when I am ill, I am unable to enjoy or muster any enthusiasm for them.

I think one of the things my husband and I have in common is a good sense of humour. We sometimes look back at events that have happened when I have been ill and are able to appreciate them for what they are. It all seems like theatre, somehow. The way that I behave when I am ill is just not me. So when we look back, we can see the humorous side of my behaviour, which is totally out of character.

I'd just like to take this opportunity of thanking him for being my nearest and dearest. Stewart, I love you.

Margaret

A PERSONAL VIEW

Personally, I do not 'suffer' mental ill health. I have it, just as someone might have red hair. I am not a sufferer!

There are times when I thoroughly enjoy being manic-depressive: it gives me my creativity, and my ability to work tremendously hard. Those who don't have these bonuses are disadvantaged. There are still the times when I am lethargic and unable to get my act together just like everybody else, whether they have a diagnosed psychiatric problem or not.

I argue that to 'suffer' mental illness is to make it a burden and not to see the advantages of the state of mind. There is a book called 'Impressive Depressives', which lists famous people of the past who have exhibited characteristics of manic depression - artists, poets, writers, and politicians. Recently the film 'A Beautiful Mind' described the schizophrenia of a Nobel Prize winning mathematician. Would these people have achieved what they did without their conditions? What I liked about the film was that the main character learned to come to terms with his illness despite the frequent intrusion of voices.

I take ownership of my manic depression. Inherited from my father's father, it belongs to me and is part of my personality. I have individual needs because of my illness and I am not afraid to declare these when necessary. I organise my life so that the symptoms are minimised. I take care with medication and I am a regular at a health club. I use complementary therapies when required, I am now nearing the end of a degree course in Fine Art taken over twice the normal number of years (one of my individual needs is to reduce pressure by not trying to do too much in a day - otherwise the next day my head may be spinning). Would I have had the chance to undertake my own personal art therapy course if I had not manic depression? Unlikely! I would be plodding on in my career chosen 30 years ago without any real thought of all the other possibilities the world had to offer.

Being positive about the manic depression is nearly always hard but I still argue, even when feeling down, that I do not 'suffer' the illness. I cope with it just as if I had frizzy red hair. To "suffer" it is to be beaten by it.

CCT

PASSING TIME

Time can either speed by or slow up
When you mature and grow up.
When time seems to speed by
It's usually when you are happy and high,
But, when time seems to go oh so slow
That normally means you're bored or full of woe.
The secret to avoid boredom and depression
And for time to pass in a steady progression
Is to get the right amount of stimulation,
Without being propelled into manic elation.
What I've just written is nothing new,
You just have to find what works for you.
I personally enjoy writing poems in rhyme
To pleasantly, poetically pass my time.

Jim Wilson

CAN'T EXPLAIN

1

Keep keep keep waiting
making the best
of it ****

sleep sleep sleep taken
no rest no best a test

no cope no cope hoping
floating
drowning
brave
weak

2

I undress the stress
stress stress stress
it is the undressing
stressing stressing me out
deprivation deprivation elation
of nothing beyond
stress stress stress
emotion stations
no entry to the gates
no access-stress stress

no inside of the outside
deprivation hours stress
deadlock.

Anon

A DIARY OF MY MOODS

by Linda Cusick

I've been going up and down for years!

It all started with the mushrooms. I came to realise that they were the source of all power and they were communicating with me. I went for endless walks in the woods and found many different varieties. Actually, I didn't just find them, they found me!

When I came out of hospital I became really depressed and I've been going through these extremes ever since with hardly any gaps between.

September

Yet another intense and painful mood swing. I felt so down, suffering and despairing thinking it would never end, then suddenly into hyper-activity and happiness and everything. I can't remember it all.

December

Just when things were beginning to settle I started to get a bit high. I had extreme emotional outbursts. I felt everything really strongly and I was so excited. I thought I might burst! My doctor says "be careful and think twice before you do anything," but I'm thinking strange and dangerous things. I'm not sleeping much. I'm too busy!

January

I'm in hospital again. Rushing thoughts and feelings of totally delicious happiness and laughing. I'm really okay now, I don't need any drugs.

February

Down, exhausted, miserable, tearful, it's hopeless. One of my drugs has made me put on three stone in weight so now I'm ugly too.

May

I threw a jam jar and smashed it. After that I wasn't able to concentrate because I felt I was being watched and I caught glimpses of insects and lots of shouting in my head. Thank goodness this is over now.

August

I dread living. It's like torture. I don't remember it being as bad as this before (but my family tell me I always say that when I'm depressed). My peace of mind has completely gone again when only a little while it came back and life was so easy.

May

I'm still depressed, mentally and physically exhausted.

June

It's happened - I'm happy again! I can do everything now and more besides. It's so funny how all this keeps happening to me.

October

A long time depressed and dreading everything, then suddenly it went away and now I feel great. I have energy, positive thoughts and happiness.

April

I'm wondering what happened since November. I know I was agitated and I couldn't keep still. I imagined that terrible things were about to happen. It led to panic attacks.

May

The days have gone by. I've gone through many changes and anguish. Sometimes I get so angry sometimes, laughing and shouting, and pacing the house and garden. I feel unbearable panic and pressure. I'm in hospital again. I hate it.

July

My moods have speeded up so that I change every three days or so. I can't keep track of this. I'm losing it. Today I'm low. I don't think I can stand this.

I'm at my lowest point. I don't want to live anymore. I've been in and out of hospital all summer.

August

My consultant arranged for me to see a specialist in my type of illness and he prescribed a new drug.

October

After taking the new drug for two months, I got better. It's like magic! I am really well now and hope it lasts this time.

April

It didn't last. I got high again and the mushrooms came back. It was all an illusion. I was in hospital for a few weeks.

August

I've had a whole year struggling with rapid mood swings and horrible anxiety. Two months ago my specialist prescribed a different drug, and here I am a few weeks later feeling well! It's been six weeks now! I can't believe how good it is.

(At last the mushrooms and I seem to have come to an understanding! Although I love them and the happiness they bring, maybe they will just remain dormant now. At least until the next time. Maybe, who knows, there might not be a next time!)

Hope is a wonderful thing!

I have often been at odds with the doctors about the pointers to the severity of my illness, such as - which features suggest I am well and which suggest I am ill.

The usual approach when I am hearing voices is to discover what the content of the voices is (what they are saying) and for what part of the day they are saying it. The content of the voices may be a useful clue to delusions and the abuse/control level may say something about the severity of the experience, but I feel I can suggest a few other clues, which may not have been thought of as important indicators to severe voices. These are completely based on my own experiences. I am not sure whether psychiatrists think of voices as being a standard fixed level experience; that is to say, one which is basically the same experience for one person whenever it happens, rather than a variable experience ranging from the mild to the severe.

The clues to 'bad' or severe voices are as follows:

1. Loudness of voices. Whether they are shouting, talking or whispering. Whether they are louder than people talking in the room.

2. Where the voices appear from. Are they in the head, the ears, the room or broadcasting from afar? The longer the distance, the worse the voices.

3. Speed of words/lack of pauses. How fast are the voices talking? Are they too fast to be talked out? The faster the voices the worse they are.

4. Number of voices talking at once. Is it a single voice? Many voices is severe.

5. Thought insertion. When accompanied by the symptoms on page 110, 112 or 113 this indicates severity and is a dangerous symptom which can lead to violence.

6. Disorder of volition. The extent to which I feel controlled and act out inserted thoughts. Also indicates the severity of my voices.

7. Bizarre restricted gait. A slow measured walk with stiff arms, legs and a hunched back (not to be confused with E.P.S.E.) is a sure sign of bad voices. Facial expression - furrowed brow.

These clues may all appear together, and the more that they appear the greater the severity of the experience. The bad voices may only be present for a short time, but this can be many times more distressing than a week of constant, mild, good voices. I believe that if these guidelines were used as indicators to the severity of my symptoms, a lot of understanding and suffering could be avoided.

AN1

13/1/94

THOSE TWO DAYS

There are two days in every week about which we should not worry.
Two days which should be kept free from fear and apprehension.

One of them is yesterday with its mistakes and cares,
its faults and blunders
its aches and pains
yesterday has passed
beyond our control.

All the money in the world cannot bring back yesterday. We cannot undo a single act we said, yesterday is gone.

The other day we should not worry about is tomorrow with its possibilities. Tomorrow the sun will rise, either in splendour or behind a mask of cloud, but it will rise until it does. We have no stake in tomorrow for it is yet unborn.

This leaves only today. Daily bread, daily grace and daily strength are promised us.

It is only when you and I relive the burdens of those two awful eternities yesterday and tomorrow that we breakdown.

It is not the experience of today that drives people out of their minds.

It is the remorse or bitterness for something that happened yesterday
or the dread of what tomorrow may bring.
When I am feeling
Down and depressed
I always read this.

Sharon

2. EXPERIENCES:

2a Personal experiences

ALEXANDER

SCHIZOPHRENIC

Dear Margaret,

I was very ill when I was 13-16 years old. I did and failed all my 'O' levels. I wanted to do 100%. I thought I was someone else. I had funny feelings in the class when I was at school. I stole books and hid them in my garden. Anyway, my father stopped me from being sectioned. I was a terror at school. You couldn't get any help in those days. It was "living hell" for my parents. I used to sleep until one o'clock in the afternoon. Anyway, it's so painful to think about what happened in the past.

My Father died in 1994.

I get treatment now. I am semi-dependent. I do my own cooking, washing, vacuuming with help from my family. I couldn't have done it without the support of my family. God knows what would have happened to me without my family looking after me when I was ill. I am better now. I get proper treatment down here. I go to a Day Centre one day a week. I have plenty of motivation now. I don't have any friends at home.

Alexander

<u>DESERTED</u>

Once I had a family -
Where are they now?
Wrapped up in their own sweet world.
So I find myself unloved and unwanted.
No family to turn to in my hour of need.
My family are left in peace to enjoy their sunny days,
And I find myself left with clouds,
That I know is my illness.
I'm left to feel unwanted and unloved.
I don't fit in anymore,
And maybe the hole I feel will never be filled again.

Thank God for The Samaritans.

Anon

CHRISTINE

21 May 1998

I am 53 now. Schizophrenia developed late in life for me when I was 42. Up until then I had been a phobic. I seem to be cured of my phobias nowadays.

I wrote a poem called 'Connie' a few years ago after I came out of hospital for the second time. In it I tried to make sense of my experiences. I have schizoaffective disorder. Not much is said about this form of schizophrenia. It is a cross between manic depression and schizophrenia. I had extreme highs and lows and also thought the devil was trying to control my mind. I saw a friend with many faces. I spent most of the time in utter despair and attempted suicide twice. Repixol turned me into a zombie, but I was put on Resperidone last year and feel great now. I miss the highs though when I felt close to God.

I'm studying literature with O.U. this year and enjoying the course.

I wish you well with your book: we need a voice.

margaret mitchell

DEAR DIARY

I keep doing the same household chore all the time, and this is dusting and polishing.

I keep playing the same tape on the stereo, it's called –'Eternal - Always and Forever', and I keep relating the lyrics to myself. If they were singing 'you're no good', I would relate that to myself, when really it's only a song. This disturbs me immensely as I have got good personality traits in me. Only my relatives and friends know that I have got some kind and thoughtful points. I'm not all bad am I? Even words on the television worry me as well, so that's why I'm not listening to the radio or television much. Surely I'm not all bad! I can't seem to get motivated to do anything. On occasions I keep pacing about not knowing what to do next. At times I do not seem to care about anyone or anything, but why? Normally I do. Sometimes I feel devoid of all feelings especially for loved ones such as my daughter or my dad. I know they love me, but it doesn't seem to affect me because I feel so cold and vacant. My daughter was here the other night with me but I was feeling terrible, I was irritable and I was feeling quite depressed. I always seem to get like that in the early part of the evening. I don't know why. I feel so helpless at the moment, with a distinct lack of confidence, but why? I haven't done anything wrong. I can't help it if I suffer with depression. Gradually over the years of having a psychological illness I have got better at times thanks to my Psychiatrist and my G.P., and with the loving kindness and support from my family and friends. I don't feel suicidal, I just feel at times very unsafe in the world around me, but why I don't know. I know it's hard to know whether I am telling the truth, but if I ever lie they are white lies, not anything nasty or wicked. A lot of the feelings I get are all in my mind. They are not rational at all. I think of some dreadful things, but they are mainly directed at myself. I wouldn't hurt anyone, not physically anyway. Sometimes I might think about harming myself but that's not very often. I don't seem to want to put the television on, not even to watch programmes I normally watch. I can't seem to make my mind up about different things. At times I feel quite lonely. Also am I living in a false sense of security? I keep thinking I am a bad person and that I have a lot of enemies, but I know this is all in the mind. I think people are linking me with someone who I knew in my school days, and to be honest, I haven't seen that person since then. I keep thinking I've done something wrong, but I know I haven't.

Therapy- Something to Do.

Every morning lately, I can't seem to get myself motivated to do things such as household chores, and the thought of going out makes me feel terrible. I don't know what to do with myself, it seems all wrong but I just can't help it. Perhaps as the day wears on I will feel better about going out. When I am feeling well I don't feel like this. At the moment I feel completely lazy, but I can't help it. I don't exactly feel anxious but I can't describe the feeling. I'm not afraid of anything, it's just that I don't want to go out. I keep wanting someone to talk to.

Last Friday I needed to go out for something but I really didn't want to go. Eventually I got enough confidence to go, and when I got back I had to lie down and have a sleep because I felt so exhausted. My daughter said I have been funny about not going out before and I have been like it several times. I can't seem to watch the television very well, and what they talk about seems to distress me. In the same vein, I can't read too many books because whatever they say seems to affect me. I think it's me in the story especially if it says anything nasty. So I am trying not to watch too much television or read too many books.

Anon

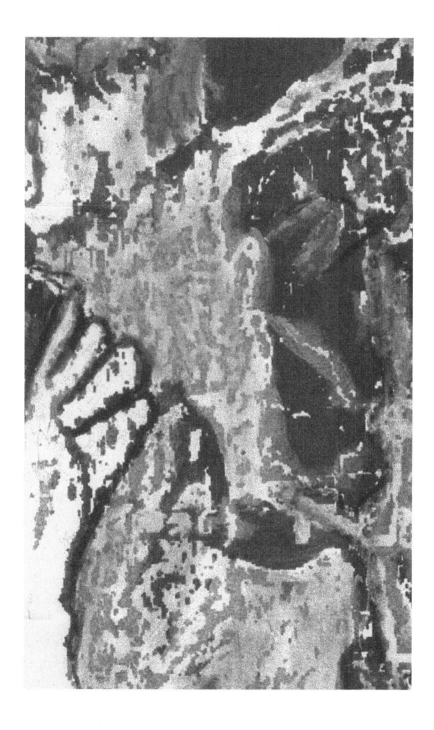

DEFEATING DEPRESSION

I have suffered from depression for 16 years, although I am pleased to say that my health has been stable for a year or two. It first started by me feeling that I was like a clock running down and needing winding up. Everything was sliding past me to a full stop. I was treated at home in my family setting and resumed my job as a teacher.

Then I became seriously ill again and ended up in hospital, being removed to a private clinic and having E.C.T. After another two admissions to private treatment and further E.C.T., I was glad that something could be done for me. Another bout led me to N.H.S. treatment in hospital, where I realised the true extent of my situation. When I was a private patient it was easy to think I was not really ill, and I felt like a hotel guest. Being in an N.H.S. hospital made me realise the true situation I was in. Two more admissions and E.C.T. led me to being put under the C.P.A. scheme, which has helped me to keep well.

It was only under this scheme that I began to come to terms with my illness, and was able to talk about how I felt and the things that happened to me. As I always withdrew into myself and cut myself off from other people I never shared my feelings of fear, anger, guilt and, most importantly of all, the feeling that I was no longer in control of my life. I cannot believe that I had visual and oral hallucinations (voices), but never told anyone. With the help of my C.P.N., I have come to accept myself as I now am.

I realised that I should leave teaching, as I was not able to take the responsibility any more, but this action has given me freedom and lack of stress. I am able to enjoy the small things of life that go unnoticed normally, and I am lucky that I can please myself and put myself first. It took me a long time to realise this was not being selfish, but necessary to my future well-being.

My experience of hospital and Clubhouse has taught me that we are all human beings and need the same love and care, something that unfortunately not everyone gets. I feel grateful for all the medical help I have had, and am still having. When one realises one's vulnerability, one is able to rebuild life in a way that can help everyone. I know that I cannot be in control of every aspect of my life, but my faith in God was reinforced through this experience as He held me up when I was weak and helpless. My family were wonderfully supportive but it reached the stage when they could do nothing but be there. I am so thankful that my husband did not desert me, as he could have done.

I feel I have been given a new start in life, and if I can learn from my mistakes I can perhaps stop myself from relapse. I know this is in God's hands and that whatever happens He will be with me, but I would like to help other people in some way.

Change is sometimes necessary, but one has to have the wisdom to know what can and cannot be changed.

Sue Cosh

EILEEN

I tried to become a Christian, and went mental instead. A spirit ruled my body and told me so many wicked things were going on. Then I attended an evangelical mission, and the preacher said, "Even that which you have I shall take away." It was all taken; my husband committed adultery, and my home was sold, because I thought I saw my husband 'cold and hungry'. Instead he was living with a girl half his age, and then my only child left to live with him because Mum was religious.

For six years, I was living off half of the home money, until it was all gone. I repented to the Lord with all my being, as Revelations in the Bible petrified me.

I became Vegetarian the Fruitarian, and ended up six stone. My daughter came to find me and I didn't even recognize her, as she was now 20. A few weeks later, a Christian vegetarian said, "Go home to your daughter." I did the next day, and in a few weeks I was put into a mental hospital. So here I am seven years on; I have my own council flat, and my daughter is a single mum to my lovely two-and-a-quarter-year-old granddaughter. I've now got osteoarthritis, but I'm coping. I'm sad that we've so little family. I was an orphan since three years old when both my parents died of T.B. in the same year. I've two sisters who I was not brought up with. They are happily married and get on with their own lives. I am still a vegetarian, and proved that by eating only fruit I could feed the world. But I proved useless and just got called schizophrenic. I do voluntary work now for Oxfam as it is the nearest way I can help world orphans. I'm sad Christians eat meat. I could cope with them eating fish and lamb at Passover. I wish everyone who ate meat had to do time working in a slaughter house. It may stop the cruel and selfish ways of man and woman.

If I was a cow, sheep, chicken or turkey, I wouldn't want to end up in a slaughter house. Oh man so needs to repent, because at Judgement we will all be answerable for our deeds.

So I was glad I had everything taken away to learn that things of the world are important, and that people are important. Sadly, few teach repentance, and if as a child I had been given my plain holy robe and not school uniform I may have turned to the Lord earlier. Sadly, I still do not know who on Earth is the father to the fatherless. Do you? Because how many are fatherless today? Millions lose parents when younger or old. I don't know where the father to the fatherless is, or what he is doing, but I wish I could find him. As he did nothing for me as an unhappy child, my foster-aunt used to always say to me, "you'll end up in the Loony Bin." I did, and then all I had was taken away. Isn't it fearful what comes to pass? Well, it cannot get worse, surely. At least I'm free of the mental hospital, and living happily, yet I get such lovely moments.

IN THE BEST
INTERESTS OF THE CHILDREN

I have watched a film called 'In the Best Interests of the Children'. It was a good film based on a true story about a woman who is a sufferer of manic depression. She had five children and lived on her own, apart from the occasional live-in boyfriend.

She found herself living on her own with her five children when she became ill and had to go into hospital. The children found it hard to accept that her behaviour was due to an illness. In the time leading up to her hospital stay she turned against her brother and his wife, who knew she wasn't well. Her brother and his wife tried to help in a way that, I too, would have felt the same way about if I'd been ill. Her brother's wife alerted the Social Services and lavished gifts on her children. I think I would have felt they were just trying to get me out of the way and were trying to manipulate the children by buying them lots of presents at Christmas. She responded by throwing her and all the children's presents back at them. I would have felt very hurt. I would have felt they were pushing me out and trying to take my children away from me. She went into hospital on the agreement that her brother didn't look after the children. The children went to live with foster parents, who came to love them very much, but they turned the children away from their mother, saying she was no good. So then the children were taken away and went to live with other foster parents. The mother ran away from hospital and ended up at her brother's. Her brother was able to make her understand that he cared for all of them, including her, and so she agreed to the children living with him and his wife. The children weren't happy at first as they didn't understand why he hadn't looked after them in the first place. The mother admitted it was her fault as she was ill at that time and disallowed it. The children then went to live with their Uncle, and that is how the film ended. Their Mother often visits them all.

I think the thing with manic depression is that it is hard for the sufferer to appreciate they are ill. The children just took it as her behaving oddly. I think as a manic depressive's behaviour can be so unpredictable, it is hard for people to know what is the best course of action to take at that moment in time. Calling the Social Services is a good step, as it is only a professional who knows the best way to assess a sufferer's behaviour and deals with it accordingly. A member of the family will possibly have no or little knowledge of how to deal with a manic depressive sufferer when they are going through a bad time, and through their concern they may make the situation a lot worse. A professional treats the sufferer's behaviour as an illness, where a carer may treat it as a well person behaving badly, and the repercussions of that may be disastrous.

Margaret

REMEMBERING

I wrote this when my funding was secure for a while and it became safer for me to allow my feelings and memories to come more to the surface. I had the safety of dealing with them in therapy with Jan. This is how remembering is - like being constantly haunted by a bad shadow.

I wake in the morning
Leave the nightmare behind
A new day has begun
But he's there in my mind.

I crawl out of bed
Rubbing my eyes
Shake him out of my head
But he's there in disguise.

I stand in the shower
I scrub myself clean
It's never enough
For where I've been.

I pull on my clothes
I brush my hair
He's there in the mirror
I remember the stare.

I walk to the kitchen
I pick up the post

Pour milk on the cornflakes
And butter the toast.

I switch on the kettle
Turn on the TV
And just for an instant
It's him that I see.

I'm sipping my coffee
Drinking it slow
Fighting off pictures
From long, long ago.

I've eaten my cornflakes
I've scraped out the bowl
Filled the hole in my stomach
But not in my soul.

I'm washing the dishes
I'm cleaning the sink
I turn up the music
So loud I can't think.

But he seeps through my body
Creeps into my brain
I know he's a ghost
But I still feel the pain.

Then it's bedtime at last
And I'm hugging my bear
Like a child in the dark
When there's nobody there.

And I wake in the night
From a terrible dream
I open my mouth
To let out the scream.

But no sound is heard
Not a cry, not a shout
But I wish I could scream
Till I'd screamed him all out.

5th May 1997   Jacqueline Monger

SANITY MADNESS AND THE FAMILY

Stage in blackness. Spotlight on inquisitor's face. Have you anything to say in your defence?

I think it took courage to walk into the fashion boutique and purchase the lingerie. And I think I had considerable luck in having chosen the right size. I agree that clambering onto the roof of my parents' house, wearing the stuff, and waving at the passers-by, was an act of extravagant lunacy. Let's face it, there can only be one reaction to a man on a roof in sheer stockings and suspenders, waving at people in the street.

In fact, this had been a part of a larger overall plan. The acts of madness appear to be odd, but they are not without reason. It's just that the reasons for these acts are a little more complicated than we are used to dealing with.

And so it was in this case. Aware of the guilt that had built up since purchasing the lingerie, the spectre of an exorcism, a somewhat gross exorcism, appeared. Suitably clad, the route up to the roof from his room, downstairs to the front door, across the street to some neighbours, back into the house and down to the bonfire patch at the bottom of the garden, described the sign of the cross. The part from the bedroom to the bonfire was to be accomplished carrying some soft-pornographic magazines: he was to offer these to the neighbours opposite (he had always felt them to be rather secretive people). They would decline, and that would be the end of the matter.

What he had not bargained on was the fact that this course of action would attract more than a little attention. As it happened, his brother realised that something was amiss when he crossed the hall dressed as a sex kitten and carrying a bundle of Playboy magazines, and managed to restrain him from going out.

This was a blow. Better no plan at all than a frustrated plan. He knew that the game was finally up, and the doctor, the ambulance, or, worse still, the police, would be round in no time. He thought the best course of action therefore was to retreat to his room. Unfortunately, there was no key to the door, so there followed an embarrassing tussle. The family G.P. could not turn it, enter the room and 'certify' him if he protested all the time, in the calmest of possible voices, that everything was all right, there was nothing amiss, and that he could go home now.

Unfortunately, there were no takers for this line of argument, and everyone felt they would have a better night's sleep if the sex kitten was removed and placed under whatever kind of restraint the local shrink felt to be necessary. This turned out to be a massive dose of something or other, and the dispatch of his clothes to a locked cupboard.

He didn't know what kind of sleep his family had that night, or about the people who had rung up during the 'incident' to complain about a man on the roof dressed in ladies' underwear (that was surely a first, the telephone call), but he remembered. Perhaps it was the first effects of the drug, rolling around in bed in fits of laughter at images of the tattered and battered bodies in the hospital around him.

Between the laughing fits, he would lie so still that the sheets began to pain his feet where they were taut at the bottom, and he would lie there making the pain increase, hoping (it sounds a little bit too altruistic. I know) that somebody else's pain somewhere in the hospital would be relieved thereby.

The next day (for some reason for he would not have done this at home) he invented a game to while away the morning hours. This involved stripping naked, emptying a litter bin, placing it over his head and dancing at the open door of his room, risking the arrival of a nurse, or, more embarrassing, a char. This, in fact, did not happen, and, becoming bored with this game of chance, he devised a game involving strength and stamina and, after a while, not a little pain. Both these pursuits, it should be added, were preferable to sitting around the television with a host of staring madmen watching the snooker or the siege of the Iranian consulate, which was then in progress.

The new game involved going into the toilet with his razor, shaving, going to the toilet and standing on his head against the wall, before flushing the loo and leaving the toilet. Now what made the game interesting was not that it had to be repeated at say five or ten minute intervals during the morning, but he would have to stand on his head several times while in there. It was a sort of self-competition. Nothing much was noticed. He had a very sore head, a sore bum and a sore face, but, finally, sitting down, exhausted, to watch the snooker, he had achieved something. And the other inmates had been just sitting there watching telly all morning, really. A nurse had asked him why he was always in the toilet and she seemed satisfied with his reply. He'd forgotten what the excuse was, but he thought it would have been nice if it had been delivered while standing on his head. The nurse in charge of the pill trolley noticed that the top of his scalp was bleeding as he lowered his head to swig back the dolly mixture, but, as he pleaded complete ignorance of the fact when asked what he had done, he was just given some ointment and the matter was forgotten, though he felt sure at the time that a note had been put on his file, and probably to his detriment.

Anything other than sitting in front of the television or playing Scrabble, I'm afraid, was definitely classed as outré. It was easy to accumulate black marks. Even lying on your bed was unacceptable if done to excess. Was it possible to lead, or to pretend to lead, a normal life in those abnormal surroundings? Most people need more than all day television and Scrabble and a host of unusual people to keep them going. He soon perceived that the pretence of normality was impossible. As soon as you walked onto the ward, and he even found these years later returning to the ward, it was impossible to tell the difference between a patient, and a doctor or a visitor. It was impossible once you went onto the ward as a patient to be anything other than a patient. From day one until the last day, you were mad, and there really wasn't very much you could do about it.

Is it surprising, therefore, that once 'inside', you became madder? He must have accumulated quite a few black marks during his stay. He had already noted the waste basket and toilet episodes. The fact that these went undetected must have meant a degree of remission both in terms of the length of his stay and the size of the dose of dolly mixture. Added to these could be mentioned dancing, once attempted with his psychiatrist, apparently meaningless gestures and movements, pretending to be part of a service hit squad which was to be planted in Northern Ireland via a psychiatric unit there (he had been much struck by the uniform, and therefore, he assumed, from the Civil Service lettering throughout the unit and the hospital he imagined an identical unit out there), as well as escaping in a dressing gown, cold baths, calling his psychiatrist a spotty faced toad, telling a patient to stand up straight when talked to, and falling deeply in love with one of the nurses.

What was the reason behind such acts? It was always a form of self-competition. If you sat around doing nothing your fortune would run out, and in order to ensure that your fortune didn't run out, you had to keep doing things. Little acts of daring. Daring because they were unusual, original, self-conceived, abnormal, socially unacceptable. They had to be witnessed, or at least if they were witnessed that increased the daring. The reward would be greater.

To this day he has not fully extrapolated this form of reasoning, hasn't really understood it. He said earlier that the actions that people classed as those of a madman were not necessarily irrational. The reasoning behind them, and there was often much reasoning and heart-rending consideration and debate, was difficult to comprehend. No one bothered to ask, of course. During the whole of the course of his illness no-one, not even a doctor, asked him what made him act like he did.

Did they not feel competent to deal with any answer that might be forthcoming? Was it thus that once someone had decided that you were ill, you were destined to remain that way until the requisite treatment had been applied? Why didn't they try and treat him, his family? Why did they just keep repeating the words 'treatment, 'treatment, 'treatment'? The same with the doctors, the only rational question he remembers being asked during his 'treatment' apart from 'does the medicine make your mouth dry', was 'did you use the pornography for sexual gratification?' No one showed the slightest interest in the illness apart from it <u>being</u> an illness.

Now, in a way, I don't blame them for this. If they'd spent hour after hour with each patient talking about his illness in a cogent manner, they would probably have treated a fraction of those who passed through the hospital. But weren't they just a little bit curious, aren't they and his family just a little bit curious now, either about what was going on in his mind at the time or about what could have caused him to act in the way he did? Why has no one ever bothered to ask? Probably because he has asked himself and he does not get a simple answer. Probably, therefore because it is too difficult, too odd, too unusual an enterprise to undertake. That is why he has been going to psychotherapy for a year and may continue for another two, because he thought that in that context someone might ask these questions. He is only dimly aware that this might be so to date, but he feels that the process is slightly subtler than having a needle poked in your backside once a month. It does some justice to the uniqueness of a human mind. A dose of dolly mixtures, the same dolly mixture that thousands of others have, does less than justice to this uniqueness, or if this sounds pretentious, and he knows it will to his father who has a sound belief in the purely physical basis of the illness (compare this with Wittgenstein's view that mental illness could be no more that 'a change of character'), you could use the word 'individuality'. He definitely disliked this seemingly crude tampering with something that any layman could be certain in calling fragile, complex and, why not, unique.

08.04.90   Anon

SOMETHING AND NOTHING

Something you left
Something you lost
Something I saved
Something I found
You and I were something
Something we were
Something you said
Something I heard
Sometimes
Nothing tries to take over
Something
You left
You lost
- Nothing

Nothing you left
Nothing you lost
Nothing I saved
Nothing I found
You and I were nothing
Nothing we were
Nothing you said
Nothing I heard
Sometimes
Something takes over
Nothing
You left

You lost
- Something

Audra Gardner

.

TALK TO THE INSTITUTE OF NEUROLOGY DR. FRITH'S CONSCIOUSNESS GROUP

In Lewis Carroll's 'Alice's Adventures in Wonderland', the following exchange occurs between Alice and the Cheshire Cat.

"What sort of people live about here?" asks Alice.

"In <u>that</u> direction." the Cat said, waving his right paw round, "lives a Hatter. In <u>that</u> direction," he said, waving the other paw, "lives a March Hare. Visit either you like. They're both mad."

"But I don't want to go among mad people," Alice remarked.

"Oh, you can't help that," said the Cat, "or you wouldn't have come here."

Alice didn't think that proved it at all; however, she went on. "And how do you know that you're mad?"

"To begin with," said the Cat, "a dog's not mad. You grant that?"

"I suppose so," said Alice.

"Well, then," the Cat went on, "you see, a dog growls when it's angry, and wags its tail when it's pleased. Now <u>I</u> growl when I'm pleased, and wag my tail when I'm angry. Therefore, I'm mad."

The Cheshire Cat is not without, to use a word beloved of psychiatric nurses, 'insight'. He gives some kind of explanation, even if one founded on the cheap logic which is perhaps characteristic of the illness, as to why he is mad. It used to rankle with me in hospital when, discussing the progress of my illness, it was suggested that I lacked 'insight'. It seemed to me then a deliberately psychiatric, rather than everyday, expression, which had the effect of reinforcing the sense that there was a fundamental difference in kind between being well and being ill. On the one hand, it seemed to say that the purported lack of insight was something most characteristic of being ill, and at the same time that the quality of insight was not the most characteristic feature of normal people. The characterisation was lopsided. Had the words self-awareness, self-reflection, self-consciousness been used, then it would have reflected belief in a line of continuity between the ill and the normal.

It may be the most difficult thing to do, to make allowance for, or give credence to, the self-reflective faculty of another's mind. We are used to, and most capable of, dealing with what a person does and says, the outcome of his thought, not the process of the thought itself. So if a person's outward expressions of thought are bizarre, illogical, unpredictable, it is perhaps natural to think there is something amiss with the thought process and therefore to focus our attention, rather bizarrely when you think about it, on that of which we have no direct experience or evidence. This is not the place to examine why I sometimes feel my treatment to have been wide off the mark, but I think there might be much to be gained, certainly personally, from looking for some kind of meaning or relevance in these outward expressions. What I believe those who experience mental illness 'from the outside' think is chiefly missing in such people, is a quality of self-awareness; that there is a kind of one-dimensional quality about the thinking, which makes the connection between thought and expression unreflectively abrupt.

A friend of mind cannot understand how one can be mad. "Weren't you aware of what you were doing?" he asks. "Weren't you aware of yourself?"

The answer is very simple. I don't believe that, even when my acts and expressions were at their most bizarre, I lacked self-consciousness or self-awareness. Rather, as I hope to describe later on, it was overridden, or rather, employed by, some stronger intention or imperative. I know how difficult it is to grasp the complete unknowability and power of the self-reflective quality of other people's minds, for I myself confronted with someone behaving apparently irrationally, immediately think that they are, in some way, unaware of themselves. I felt this of the other patients on the ward; that in some way the power of reflection to mediate between our thought and our action had been diminished, that a facade of self-consciousness had been lifted, that they were in personality what they thought and felt inwardly, transparent, one-dimensional.

To wish to be, to act out 'out there' what was going on inside my head, was one characteristic of my thinking. It was often necessary to say or do the first thing that came into my head: to strike while the iron was hot, to capture the pristine quality of the idea by revealing it to the outside world, or acting it out. To fail to act on such 'first inspiration', as I would call them, was to fail, to the extent that utterance or performance at the second prompting would mean a less favourable result for myself, and not expressing them at all could mean a very bad result indeed. For me, this element of the dare, the challenge, was perhaps one of the most characteristic and frightening features of my illness. Once the idea to do or say something was in the head, however small the prompting, the challenge became to act on it, and the quicker one acted upon it the greater the reward. Hence, I got off a bus one evening on the way to the cinema and, with what I stood up in, spent two days and nights walking down to Hungerford. Hence, I climbed, somewhat dangerously, onto the roof of my parents' house and waved at the passers-by. Hence, I crawled around the streets where I lived, on my hands and knees, for an hour and more. Hence I spent an entire morning, while in hospital, doing handstands in the loo. Promptings which had to be obeyed, or the result would be worse for me, but if obeyed at the first suggestion, then the reward would be great. (None of the rewards was ever realised, I might add.)

Where was the self-consciousness, the self-awareness in such acts? To some extent it was there because to have lacked these qualities would have made the acts less difficult. It was just because one was aware that they were unusual, embarrassing, bizarre, that they had just that right quality of difficulty to make them worth doing. If one had been unaware of the difference between normality, and one's unusual project, they wouldn't have been worth doing. Not a very sophisticated or useful quality of self-awareness, you might say. But it was almost as if self-awareness had to be overcome by appeal to some higher logic, some solipsistic game plan: the challenge, as it came to me, required immediate performance. A kind of getting one's thoughts out into the open in performance. A kind of bodying forth of consciousness into the outside world.

Freud wrote that, "when a neurasthenic describes his pain, he gives an impression of being engaged in a difficult task, to which his strength is quite unequal. He is clearly of the opinion that language is too poor to find words for his sensations and that these sensations are something unique and previously unknown, of which it would be quite impossible to give an exhaustive description." I feel something of this difficulty myself. I have tried to describe one characteristic of my thinking when I was ill. It is very difficult to summarise the heterogeneity of the experiences. They are, of course, as Freud suggests, no more unique than any other person's experiences, but they are possibly more nebulous, fragmentary, without continuity. The process of acting on impulse, as I have described, was possibly an attempt to pin down, or fix something which was fleeting: to bring thought out into the real world, make it tangible, real.

Anon

THE WAY I SEE IT

by Jenny Porteous

I can clearly recall my first experience of mental illness, although at the time I had no idea what it was, and in fact the term 'mental illness' was not a part of my vocabulary at all. I was working in a large telecommunications factory and living nearby. On the day it all began, I went back to my lodgings for dinner as normal. It was a Friday, which meant fish and chips were on the menu, my favourite. After lunch, the rest of the family got ready to return to work, but I was stopped by my landlady saying she wanted to have a word with me. Wondering what I may have done wrong, I waited until the others had left when she told me to sit down, and, to my surprise, asked what was wrong with me. "Nothing" I replied, as far as I was concerned there was nothing wrong, or at least nothing that I could put my finger on. When she asked me if I was sure, I promptly burst into tears, and all I could say was that I didn't know what was wrong with me. That evening my landlady went with me to see the doctor, and that was the beginning of endless visits to psychiatrists, psychologists, therapists, and goodness knows who else! It was also the start of my treatment which, over the years, has included all kinds of pills, injections and electric shock treatment. I seemed to be spending more time in the local mental hospital than at home, and no one ever gave me any real explanation as to what was wrong with me. Terms like 'personality disorder', 'inferior complex' and even 'schizophrenia' started to creep into the conversation, and I was very frightened indeed. I felt I was going round in an endless circle and there seemed to be no way out.

However, things took a turn for the better about ten years or so ago. That was when I finally realised that I had to do something to help myself. Until then I had wrongly been expecting some kind of magic cure from the doctors. Medication, support and counselling, therapy etcetera are all very important in mental health care, but if the patient is unwilling, or unable to make full use of these services, while making every effort to get well, there is little the doctor can do. That was an extremely hard lesson I had to learn, and it took an awful long time, many years, to learn it.

Agoraphobia is one of my biggest difficulties, but with the help of books, cassettes, and a good support worker it is controllable, and I have gradually learned to face and deal with my fears. I even enjoy going shopping, having coffee in the cafe and meeting people, everyday things that seemed almost impossible a few years ago. Recently, I have taken up relaxation and meditation, which I find very helpful. I'm also trying to change my outlook to life in general by being more positive, trying not to get het-up over little things. It isn't easy, but is well worth the effort to make life better. Although I still have a lot of very bad times, I have managed to stay out of hospital for almost fifteen years now.

Looking back on more than thirty years of mental health problems, I wonder where the time has gone. Sometimes I ask myself if things could have been different, but don't we all? Looking to the future, I feel more confident than I have for many years; maybe there is a bit of uncertainty, but surely that is the same for all of us. I am fortunate to have a great team of people on my case, and they give me all the help and support they can, without which I would probably be back to square one, so thank goodness for care in the community.

This picture was painted by Linda, was when she was experiencing a 'high' at the time. She felt it represented three green creatures with black tails that could be aliens tapping into her power.

BUDGIE AND HAMSTER

I remember once when I was ill, I think I felt that it was the end of the world, and that we had passed from life and into heaven. I went into my daughter's bedroom and I decided the budgie and the hamster should not be left in their cages as everyone was now free, so I left their cage doors open for them to escape. Apparently the cats were in the house, but fortunately my husband was at home and he managed to recapture the hamster and budgie before they came to any harm.

Margaret

FULL POTENTIAL?

How, as a mental health sufferer, can I reach my full potential? I was doing well in maths studying for a GCSE when bang, hey presto, illness hits me, and I end up in hospital. When I try again I find I have forgotten so much that I am nearly back to square one. It's as if I get carried away with the enjoyment and satisfaction of the possibility of fulfilling my ambitions, when hey presto, I start becoming too high, it's all too much, and I end up in hospital. My life is full of unfulfilled dreams, hopes and lost aspirations. Back to square one is my theme tune.

Margaret

LARGER THAN LIFE

I remember once when I was ill I found that my faith became larger than life. I remember one time when I was ill that it felt as if it was coming to the end of life and the beginning of heaven. I remember I went out into the garden. It was dark, and my husband closed the door to the garden. I felt as if God had locked me out in the wilderness. I quickly rushed to the door and got into the house. I remember my husband helping me to cook the dinner. We had meat in the oven, vegetables and spuds in saucepans. When we bought the vegetables and spuds to the boil, it felt as if it was a kind of judgement day. The vegetables and spuds represented the people who were alive, all the bad people being disposed of.

Anon

MISTRUST

I remember once when I wasn't well, my husband, Stewart, and I went to see the doctor, and he prescribed some tablets. That evening, Stewart gave me a cup of coffee with the tablets. I was engrossed in the television, but when I realized he wanted me to take tablets, I panicked and thought he was trying to give me what I suppose I saw as poison. I had forgotten all about seeing the doctor. I saw he had given my daughter, Michelle some sweets, which I thought could be tablets. I tried to get them out of her mouth. Stewart tried to get me to take the tablets. This is all I can remember.

Margaret

SAFE WITH CLIFF

I remember one time when I wasn't well, I was at a stage when I didn't feel very safe with my husband. We went for a walk to the village, and I said I would just pop into the newspaper shop. When I got into the shop I panicked, and felt that it was my opportunity to get away from him. So I sneaked out of the shop and went home. I was frightened, so I closed all the curtains and locked the doors. When my husband arrived home and wanted to be let in I phoned the police. When they arrived I let my husband and the police in. I switched on the Cliff Richard cassette, which I called 'my friend'. Cliff Richard made me feel secure. We all had a cup of tea and a chat. The police were very nice and after they felt all was well, they left us to it.

Margaret

SAFE

I remember when I wasn't well and we were decorating the lounge. We had made the dining room into a temporary lounge/diner. There weren't enough sockets for all our gadgets, so Stewart fitted a temporary extension lead with a double socket. This worried me. He was a very competent electrician, but could I trust him? Had he made it safe? My level of illness made me doubt the motives of my loved ones. To be sure, I decided I would check out the extension lead. I took it to an electrical store. They checked it out and said it was fine. My faith in human nature had been restored. Stewart wasn't such a bad guy.

Margaret

THE CAR

Once when I was ill I drove the car into town. When I was returning home, I could smell fumes in the car. I thought my husband had rigged the car so the fumes would kill me. I stopped the car and left the door open and walked the rest of the way home. When my husband came home, he asked what the car was doing with the door left open down the road. I felt embarrassed. He went and brought the car home.

Margaret

WIRED FOR SOUND

When I was in hospital, my daughter had become distressed at my behaviour due to my illness (unknown to me), so she felt she was unable to come and visit me or talk to me on the phone. I became very agitated that I was not able to have any contact with Michelle. I didn't understand why (as I saw it) my family were keeping her from me. So I decided enough was enough, and it was time for me to go and find her. So I put on my cardigan, trainers and personal stereo, I had Cliff's 'Stronger' album playing (at this point in time I was really into Cliff Richard) and I set out to find out what was going on with regard to my daughter. There I was, walking, listening and singing along with Cliff. I really got a buzz out of it all, and I felt free! People seemed to smile at me, perhaps they approved of my singing!

My first port of call was my mother-in-law's bungalow. It was about a mile from the hospital. She wasn't in, so I left a flower on her doorstep. I then made the trek home, about five miles in all from the hospital. As it happened, my husband was on his way home, and he passed me near our home, so he was able to greet me when I reached home. I remember that I didn't trust him. He offered me a cup of tea, and I insisted on having milk from an unopened pint of milk. I thought he may have tampered with the milk and that he might be trying to poison me (how neurotic can you get). Whilst I was there I asked about Michelle. He told me she was staying with a friend, so I phoned her at her friends. I was so relieved to speak to her and know for myself that she was okay. Stewart phoned the hospital and they said they would arrange for transport to take me back to the hospital. I wasn't going to trust

Stewart to take me back. Before I left, I put Cliff Richard's album on, called 'The Album', and I remember for some reason feeling that Cliff wanted me to pack up all my memorabilia into a suitcase and take it with me to the hospital. When I arrived there I remember finding it hilarious that I had so much stuff that I filled up a whole suitcase!

I remember I used to play Cliff's music and then later, when other people had had their music on for quite a while, I would threaten them that if they didn't do this or that, I would play Cliff's record! I think some of them liked his music, but I guess I just played it too much, and in their eyes they could have too much of a good thing!

Margaret

WHERE IS CLIFF?

One time when I was ill I kept listening to Cliff Richard's albums and I really thought that I was the one that he was singing to, as I picked up through the lyrics things that could relate to myself. I didn't hear voices as such, but I have a river down the road from where I live. I didn't hear voices as such, but I remember thinking he was keeping an eye on me, that he was in a helicopter up in the sky and I felt guided by my own imagination. I felt he wanted me to walk in to town. I ended up in a park where it felt as though he wanted me to take off my shoes and leave all my possessions behind. So I left my coat, shoes and bag on a park bench. When no helicopter landed to pick me up I felt very unsettled and disturbed, so I walked without my possessions, just a Cliff Richard key ring, to a nearby pub. They could see I wasn't quite right. They kindly gave me a sandwich and asked me for my phone number. At first I just gave them my Cliff Richard key ring, then I came to a bit and told them my phone number. The police came and took me to the local hospital where my psychiatrist and husband were. I was angry with my husband. I soon calmed down and was taken for a stay in hospital. Fortunately a gentleman had handed in my bag to the police and my possessions were still where I left them.

Margaret

YOU ARE NOW FREE

Whenever I am on a high I usually believe that it will soon be the end of the world and that heaven will take over. One time I walked into town and I was in the toilets. When I was washing my hands, this lady was in there, and she had a placard which read 'You are now free'. It felt as though she was an angel from heaven, and I didn't like to say anything to her, but it made me feel as though the message was for me, and that I would soon be going to heaven. When I was walking home I saw some road signs which said something like 'the end', and I thought it would be the end of this life when I passed the sign, but when I did I remember nothing had happened, and then it made me feel rather insecure and a bit frightened.

Margaret

THE BEGINNING

I think it is maybe better for me to start at the beginning. This will give a basic history of where things went wrong for me, with regards to the possibility that your early life can influence the way mental illnesses are created. Everyone is unique and the causes are different for every user or survivor. If there were a standard to go by, then life would be made easier. A 'cure', maybe.

My experiences relate to my early life. At home, up to about eight or nine years of age, my elder brother and father taught me that you had to be aggressive or tough in life to earn respect. So I was literally kept on a lead, like a pet dog, taught to use aggression to hit other people or children. It did not matter how old or big the children were, and I did not need provocation or reason to fight. Basically, I was rewarded like the dog. My reward was affection, which was not shown except when I 'earned' it through my actions.

The only snag with having such a life is what you are actually like inside yourself. I was very artistic (I won my first art competition at the age of seven). I enjoyed nature, reading and poetry. So I was living a double life, hiding the sensitive side to my nature because I would not earn 'rewards' for showing them.

Then at about twelve or thirteen I had my first experience of depression. I became anti-social, totally against the system. I dropped a class in school, from the 'A' class to the B' class, because of my lack of interest in school, which they saw as a lack of intelligence. The school didn't know my father had lost his job, my brother had left home to join the army, my sister had got married and left home and my dog had died. Everybody I knew of my own age group was frightened of me so they weren't really friends. It was not really talked about in the early sixties, and my parents did not tell the school anything that was going on. My local G.P. put me on Purple Hearts to calm me down, not exactly the ideal answer, but child psychologists were very few on the ground in those days. Nobody wanted to know about mental illness. It was hidden away and not talked about.

At about the same time, a local farmer sexually assaulted me. Again, everything was kept quiet and not talked about. Even the local police didn't want to know.

I joined Art College direct from school, and had to leave six months later because of family financial problems. So back to the doctors and put on some kind of tablets. I was not even told I was in a depressive state or suffering from an 'illness'.

When I was about nineteen or twenty I had my first schizophrenic experience. I kept on thinking someone was trying to suffocate me when I was sleeping, and thought that I could not sleep because I would leave my body. I was also visited by little men who kept telling me that I was an alien and I should go back to their planet. They probably call it a U.F.O. experience today. I find it quite comical really today. I wonder if they are schizophrenic, or if they have really experienced something? At about the same time, I was sleepwalking to the extent that I was even taking a shower when I was asleep.

Although through my life I have had various incidents and various 'visitors' in my brain (do I have one?) and been treated by psychiatrists, psychologists and psychotherapists, it is very rare that any have told me exactly what is wrong with me. On one occasion, I was threatened with E.C.T. to get me away from the psychiatrist who was a trainee (a doctor on a six-month stint as a psychiatrist). The consultant told him this was not the right action. This affected me and I thought all sorts of things. I went around shouting at people at every occasion, talking to myself, enjoying watching people's reactions to this, as they didn't know where to put their faces in embarrassment. The other nice little trick I did was to bash my head on bus stops, signs and so on. Again, the little people were telling me to do this, I was their agent.

This was when I was put in hospital for assessment and diagnosed as having schizophrenia. This was in Germany, and the doctors there put me on some tablets, of which one blew my head off and made me sleep, but they weren't too bad and pretty easy to use. The ones with a green band on them for daytime, the ones with the red band for night-time. I was let out after two weeks, and visited the psychiatrist about every two weeks for about six months. The psychiatrist had the time to do counselling at the same time so I got better.

I returned to England, but because my medical records were in Germany they refused to issue me with the necessary drugs that stabilised me, even though I told them about my illness. Approximately six months later. I was told I was having a breakdown, which they again diagnosed as schizophrenia. So I was issued with the appropriate tablets yet again.

Why does it take so long to get doctors or psychiatrists to believe you? Why do they seem to 'guess' and use us as guinea pigs for drugs? Why do they never tell you exactly what's wrong with you until you ask? Why do they never tell you about other services or organisations you can use for your benefit? Are they frightened of losing control, frightened of disempowerment, scared of user-led organisations? I ask how many times do you go out to a user group and actually find a so-called 'professional' who is even interested in taking part, just to find what is happening on the 'other side'? Unfortunately, it is really still 'them and us' to a great extent.

Society has labelled me to fit in the slot provided by them, and when I admit to my mental illness I find a lot of people patronise me. It is mainly because of misunderstanding, or believing all the bad events the news media portray. I am waiting for the day when the news media turn around and report all the good we can do. This would at least give a fairer picture of us.

In the borough of Greenwich where I live, the Mental Health Team of Social Services provide you with addresses of users and survivors. The Health Authority does not give you any information about groups, just the usual odd leaflets in the waiting rooms. They have yet to come to the conclusion that user groups are great self-help groups as well. The best advocates are users themselves, and when we have been in the system quite a while we literally only need the doctors to prescribe our medication. I think once you get more confident about your illness the easier it is to handle, and initially you get guilt trips. "I can, I admit" seems only to come into the brain later on. The initial response is so despondent and you think you have a badge on top of your head, telling everyone 'Hello, I am crazy', and worry a lot about what people will think.

I could carry on indefinitely over the subject of mental illness, but I will close with one small incident, which happened to me last week.

I was told by Social Security that I was no longer entitled to income support/incapacity benefit because I did not attend the all-work examination with one of their doctors. The reason I did not attend is because I never actually received a letter or form from them. So after letters going backwards and forwards, I eventually went to the Social Security Office. They said you have been classed as capable of work. I said my G.P. and psychiatrist have just given me another thirteen weeks' sick note. They said to me "Oh! It doesn't matter about that now we have classed you as capable of work." It appears now that the social security offices can decide if you are well or not. This is without medical opinions, without being assessed by a doctor at all. I went to the Law Centre here in Abbey Wood, who sorted it out for me. Apparently, they are supposed to send you the examination form or whatever it is by recorded post, and if you do not attend they are supposed to follow up with a house visit. This rule applies to all mental illness sufferers. I have never known them to move so fast. The Law Centre appealed on my behalf over the phone and it was accepted there and then. I am now back on full benefits.

The reason I quote this from Social Security is I found it very distressing and it put me on a 'down'. If this had happened a few years ago it would have made me suicidal, I am positive about that. It was proof to me that certain people still have the attitude that mental illness sufferers don't need full explanations of the reasons behind their decisions. Why are we treated at times like second-class citizens when we are normal people with sensitive feelings and needs?

Robert Hughes

WHY?

Why when I think I'm normal and having fun does everyone judge
me?
Why do I appear what I am not and when I talk they run?
Why am I so hard to understand? Can people not see me?
They talk and judge and won't let me be.

Sue

EXTENSION LEAD

One time when I wasn't well, we were decorating, and my husband
rigged up a temporary electric socket (he is an electrician). I didn't
trust him so I decided to take the extension along to be checked out
at an electrical shop. They said it was fine. Because your nearest
and dearests become so worried about you, they become agitated
by your behaviour, which comes across as aggressive, and so you
think life would be better if they could do away with you.

Margaret

MARGARET

I had a mild schizophrenic breakdown when I was in my forties. Some ten years ago, I had periods of 'unsteadiness' for a few years, when I lost weight and felt that things generally were slipping away from me. I was also, and am to a lesser degree these days, a carer, as I have two sons who suffer from the condition. Thankfully, at present the three of us are stable and able to continue living our lives.

I wrote the following piece while I was ill, which might convey some of the vulnerability that I felt:

> The yellowed surface of an ancient map
> Outlines diffused, squandered
> Flung out to the wind
> A game of chance.
>
> Outstretched hands
> With gaunt fingers
> Of a transparent hue
> Reach out of touch
> The forgotten shapes.

The clearest memories that I have were that of subjectivity, and I was dominated by the childhood experiences. My moods would swing, one minute I would laugh which would become exaggerated only to be closely followed by tremendous sadness and weeping. I was dispersed from my 'centre'.

When I was a carer I was on a low daily dosage of Sulpiride, and found some solace in evening drinking. I was sufficiently stable to live through the trauma each day. It was very difficult, and it did not help that the majority of people, including my extended family, would relate to me their own problems and those of others. The general idea was to recognise that there were others far worse off than me. In fact, it had the opposite effect a great deal of the time, because it made me feel invisible. I found it difficult to address my problems without initially recognising them.

I wrote this piece at that time - an attempt at expressing what I felt was the perversity of life:

> The wall is painted white
> It leaves no imprint of previous life
> The whiteness has absorbed all emotion
> It stands cold and clear
> Covering the dark stain
> That smashed its surface and
> Ran in rivulets to a conclusion.

I hope that maybe I have given you some help and wish you well with your book. People in similar situations to me appreciate the attention and the support that you give.

THOUGHT WAVES

Saturday the sixth of December
Was a day I think I will remember
As in the morning while I was in bed
I heard a voice come inside my head.
The voice was loud and said succinctly,
'Stop thumping' very distinctly.
It differed from a regular auditory hallucination
And was more like an intended telepathic communication.
It wasn't a neighbour shouting nearby,
It was more like a sort of reply
To one of my telepathic calls
That are usually like banging my head on walls.
I use satellites and the local radio mast
To boost the transmissions that I broadcast.
I send out messages through my mind
In a universal language to all humankind.
It is like a telepathic phone language
Which the recipient converts to their own language.
It will become more efficient than electronic mail
And is similar to the system used by a whale.
It will give free telecommunications to all,
Though phone companies' shares may fall,
You just have to remove a brick from your wall
And then practise at making a call.
So now perhaps I'm getting through
To the whole world and you,

To help to make Earth a better place
For the whole human race!

Jim Wilson

Dear ALL,

Oh what JOY? Oh what vision we see or seek in our seasonal landscape. Doctor in his joyous heaven yet stale from his fragile powers.

ROLL ON THE EIGHTH!!

How subtle was our holy shrikand? How fragrant were our toiled browse.

We seek and seek the necessary in what communion we were foresworn to take/drown. Fresh from the locks with my seven legs and no arms I study unworried by mere life rich and tapestry.

I AM SWOLLEN BUT NOT IRATE!!

We wrote to bank managers spew forth literature. I and I in Joh Jah heavenly bodies from Mars.

I re-await your formal application.
Time for a chat - TRY ME!!

LOVE,

AN5

AS FRIENDS

All my friends have all been very good to me, kind, supportive and affectionate. My relatives have been the same also, but why is it I still feel all alone and desolate like I do? The vibes given to me by friends and relatives are really telling me that they don't care at all or am I wrong, do they really? I feel so alone inside of me that I can't even give out good vibes to other people. I do love my family and friends, but how can I show them that I do? I am sorry for being the miserable, mean person that I am. I am so selfish, never thinking about other people, only about myself. I am sorry for not loving people as I should, but when I feel depressed I can't. I try to help people sometimes. I appreciate all I have either materially or otherwise. I am not a greedy person, only when it comes to food. I don't always know who is being genuinely friendly to me and also who isn't. I like to think I know who are my friends and who aren't really. I don't know what to expect anymore or what direction my life is going in. I hope it's not anything nasty. I am not perfect, but I can safely say I am a good person. I am a good person who has perhaps taken things a little bit too seriously in the past and now someone somewhere is taking advantage of me and making what was maybe a joke into a real serious event. But why? I wouldn't hurt anyone, not physically anyway. I am just a depressive trying to keep going regardless. I am my own worst enemy and I am all self all of the time. I never think of others. When I'm depressed I always get a terrible guilt complex about myself, why I don't know because I haven't done anything wrong, at least nothing that I know of. I am a good, honest person. I will admit to maybe telling a few white lies, and I know I have told my psychiatrist a few, particular things, but these are all in the mind, they're not rational thinking.

Anon

3. A WALK ON THE DARK SIDE

ANOTHER DAY TO FACE

Face the deep pain of death
Round and round in circles
Another day to <u>face</u>
The painful feelings I've inside
Simply leads me to the thoughts
of suicide.

Being labelled this and that
by insensitive people
Those who think they know it all but all they
Do is add oh more and more
From which you're left to <u>face</u>.

You nearly succeed in the end
The deep pain of death
But the long life tube goes down
Inside again and all you're left
With is another day to later
<u>face</u> once again

by Jane Newman

When there is depression all around us, it is difficult to feel the blue skies beyond the rainbow.

Daphne

I HAD A DREAM

I had this funny dream,
It's the strangest one I've ever had.

In this dream I could do just what I like,
So up I floated like a funny kite;

And I looked at the houses down below,
But now they looked like little mushrooms;
With an orange - yellow glow.

Well by now I was so very high,
It made me feel quite ill.
I lost my concentration,
Which made me start to fall.........

Faster, faster like a falling brick,
I saw the ground come rushing up
It made me feel quite sick;

And as I was about,
To hit the ground below;
A voice inside my head
        yelled "NO,"

I woke up feeling hot and cold,
And sat up in my bed;
Cause I remember people saying,

If you ever hit the ground when falling,
You'll always end up dead.

STEVE

SECOND LOVE LOST

Buy a villa in your mind
Stir the juices of your kind
Remember the night we sat and watched a star?

Later I drew out a knife
Tried to take another life
But the jazz band in my brain kept my eyes ajar.

Don't sew me no sequin divine
Let sink another brain in wine
Piece it together, sell it in some sleazy hole.

Someone stole my legs
Can't seem to take the dregs
So compromise with hate, kick a bucket, score a goal.

You must fritter your ideas
Or you stir up learned fears
Only to sweat and scream a silent mortal thought

I'll come to no harm, no,
My body's Meccano
But you will find the peace that only death has bought.

Remember the night we sat and watched a star?
A jazzband in my brain kept my eyes ajar.
Piece it together, sell it in some sleazy hole,

Compromise with hate, kick a bucket, score a goal,
Only to seat and scream a silent mortal thought
And you will find the peace that only death has bought.

Austen Cordasco

SHE BROUGHT IT ON HERSELF

One woman, no money -
She can't have much going for her.

One woman, no money, no man -
There must be something wrong with her!

One woman, no money, no man, no job -
She must have a learning difficulty!

One woman, no money, no man, no job, no family -
She must have a personality disorder.
She's terribly difficult to get on with.

One woman, no money, no man, no job, no family, no friends -
She tried to kill herself, and now she's in hospital?
I told you there was something wrong with her!
It's a good job we didn't get involved with her,
Who knows what she would have done!

One woman, OD'd. Put her in with the other losers. NEXT
PATIENT, PLEASE!

Anon

SUICIDE

Suicide: a chilling word.
People call it cruel to do,
But I'm me, not you.

Suicide: a desperate word.
Call it cowardly if you like,
But I'm scared to stay and fight.

Suicide: a lonely word.
You will never understand.
But dead I cannot hurt.

Hurt people, I don't want to hurt.

Suicide: a happy thought.
Yes, I see you disagree;
But that's you,
        Not me.

STEVE

This is the Chelmsford Samaritans

THE GRIM REAPER

Sit silently my son
as the dark of night approaches
It is but a time
Without the sun

The things of the night
cannot touch us
We have our love
to keep us safe

So walk you grim reaper
and touch those
you must but leave us alone
Our time has not yet come

Fuzz   15/1/97

THE WAY I SEE THINGS

I have been through a period of depression. I felt as if something terrible had gone irreparably wrong but could not put my finger on what. To my horror I discovered my best friend had killed herself. She was 26 years old and a Christian. She spent most of her time fighting for justice, including exposing multinational exploitation in the third world. I only saw her about once every three weeks but the conversation we had was about suicide and parenting. We both said the only thing that prevented us from taking our lives was the children. She knew how her son would feel - she found her mother dead due to suicide when she was a young teenager. We also believed that God would take it as an insult and send us to Hell.

Someone suggested to me recently that people find it easier to be down because of the gravitational plane we live on making it harder to be up and that somehow this has a fixed psychological effect on our mood patterns.

I have also had it suggested to me that since the moon controls the ocean and since each human is like the earth, two thirds water, then the moon also must logically have an effect on the individual. I know a group of women who swear by the theory, by charting their menstrual cycle according to the moon. They believe that the moon has a major significance on the mood of the individual. I do not know enough about either of these ideas to discard or accept them, but I think it would be very interesting to do some research around them.

I have enclosed a few poems that I wrote while I was down. I don't think of them highly but just thought if I had not made any sense in the Letter I have written then I may as well send some poems and make it worse, as usual! Wishing you the best of health.

Anon

4. CARERS:

4a Carers

CLARE

Our interest stems from having a daughter who commenced her problems when we moved here from the U.K. some 25 years ago. We believe this was the trigger factor, as she commenced anorexia just afterwards, and her problems escalated. There was never ANY credence given to the fact that this could have been the <u>cause</u>, in fact the first psychiatrist she ever saw categorically REFUSED to even discuss the condition and pronounce the dreaded word! We subsequently saw a specialist well versed in anorexia, who said that very often symptoms mimicked schizophrenia, but by then the damage was done and the neuroleptic path embarked upon.

Soon after that we took Clare to the U.S., where she was in the care of the psychiatrist. During our three months there, he took her off all medication and she underwent very comprehensive physical testing. This indicated that she was very biochemically imbalanced - her menstruation had ceased for some eight and a half years. She was prescribed a regime with nutritional changes, such as vitamins, on which she coped very well for eight months, but boredom set in and caffeine, nicotine and alcohol became the order of the day. (All this was in the U.K.)

Clare then went to a behavioural unit, and medication recommenced. When we showed the next psychiatrist our large dossier of results from the U.S., he laughed and talked about 'our American Health Farm' and did not even look at the dossier.

So our complaint with orthodox psychiatry is that is has a completely closed mind to complementary therapies and only seeks the pharmaceutical route. My husband and I felt so strongly about this that we talked with a few professionals who are a little more progressive and we were interested in setting up a unit. Unfortunately, our daughter became our priority and we were not able to give the time to developing these ideas although we had good feedback (I am sure funding would be forthcoming if necessary).

Clare at the moment is in a community in Devon, and has developed her cravings for caffeine despite being forbidden it, and she will do anything - literally anything - for a cup of coffee or tea. This makes her abusive and sometimes aggressive. We would like to see this more fully investigated, as coffee is available 24 hours a day in any psychiatric establishment we have visited. Again, credence is not given to the possible effects of caffeine on SOME people.

Another point - the national mental health associations do not seem to liaise with the Schizophrenia Association of Great Britain in Bangor, Wales. It was founded by Mrs. Gwyneth Hemmings, who also is convinced that there is very much a physical aspect to mental health - a healthy mind MUST have a healthy body. It seems a great shame that there is not this official liaison.

Clare's present community have asked her to leave because of her cravings - what a problem!

FROM A CARER

Looking back, it's like a four-year nightmare. A lot I don't remember, I've blocked it out. We were lucky, we have always had a good marriage. I don't know how people cope if there isn't any love.

I've seen big, strong men crying hopelessly because they could not cope with their wives being mentally ill. I found it so hard and worrying when I went out. I didn't know what to expect to find when I got back. I always hid the tablets in different places. I hid the phone because he would be phoning the doctor, which happened in the past.

Sometimes he was so bad pacing up and down the room, I was in tears. I had only to phone our children and they would have us to stay with them, which was so helpful. Our children have been so wonderful at all times. We are very blessed.

It's wonderful now he is better. It took lots of changing tablet combinations to get him well, but it has worked. Thank God, he is enjoying life once again, and so am I.

Anon

MOTHER'S LITTLE HELPER LEFT TO COPE ALONE

To be a child carer of a mentally ill parent is a difficult and often unacknowledged situation. The mental health team that take care of the adult forget that the children have needs too, which are just as immediate and important as those of the acutely or chronically ill person, and which often go unmet. Without a healthy parent to model behaviour for the child or do the caretaking necessary, the child is left to parent her/himself and may grow up with a distorted view of life and of normal adult behaviour.

In my own case, my mother has been having acute episodes of illness all my life, but was seriously ill in 1983/84 when I was 13 or 14 years old. I was there alone when she was having a psychotic episode, and had no back up when my mother was diagnosed with schizophrenia. In fact, that was a secret - I only found out the diagnosis from my sister and have spent most of my life since denying that diagnosis was true. One reason for this is that it was never talked about openly in the family. I still don't know if my uncles and aunts know what is wrong with my mother. Well-meaning parents have hidden the details from me, never allowed me to be there when she has seen her consultant psychiatrist, and no mental health worker was sent to the house to see that it was I and my older brother who were taking over the parent role for the rest of our brothers and sisters, and that my mother was not getting the help she needed from our father or any other source (her mother being dead and her father elderly, and having fallen out with her sister). Nobody sat down with us (with me) to talk to us about her illness and what that meant, or for us to ask questions. I grew up confused, and I still am confused about my mother's illness. For years, I thought that my mother's illness was my fault.

At 13, I was afraid of my mother, having seen her acutely psychotic. I didn't want her to come home from the hospital I was so afraid of her. I was glad she had to go in for another two weeks.

By the age of fifteen I was having my own panic/anxiety attacks, and was taken to the doctor by my mother. He wanted to put me on beta-blockers and pooh-poohed my request for counselling. In fact, when one of my younger brothers went to the doctor over anxiety he was told, "Oh no, not another Harris!" This is a doctor who claims mental illness is his special interest! I have mistrusted this doctor and the medical profession ever since. I have also grown up with my mother going to the doctor to have her tablets upped every time she had a problem or a crisis. I describe it to myself as 'going to get herself fixed'. I have grown up with the notion that you should go to the doctor whenever you are down. Also, that emotions are bad and must be wiped out by medication and never discussed with openness and acceptance. I am still terrified of my mother's doctor or anyone with psychiatrist or psychologist in their job title, and this is at the age of twenty-nine.

I have been seeing a psychiatrist since 1989 but have never been offered anything except mediation. I did art therapy for 18 months, which was useless. I have never been allowed to discuss my feelings about my mother or my childhood, and I am continually put on the back burner by therapists who don't want to listen. With an IQ in the top band of the population, I have been dictated to by social workers as to the appropriate "therapy" for "my situation" after ten minutes of talking to me. In fact, I think they had already decided on art therapy before meeting me. The art therapist was not approachable, and would not talk to me while I drew "whatever I was feeling" for an hour. I feel my intelligence and self-sufficiency has been blunted by not being able to talk about my problems on an equal basis, and treated like a stupid child.

You may wonder, why, if I have such intelligence, did I submit to this? I can only say that with my family background and culture, that the doctor's word was law and must be obeyed as law, and being still not much more that a child, I did what I was told.

My mother's attitude that the doctors are always right was difficult to break without any social support of my own.

While social workers have attempted to put me in touch with my feelings, I have completely lost my confidence, and have become increasingly suicidal and more and more dependent on therapists. This has resulted in a recent hospital stay, in which I was treated for psychotic episodes. I have already been on an anti-psychotic medication for three years, in an attempt to treat me for anxiety, which led to panic attacks on a daily basis. I proved this by eventually persuading a doctor to take me off this medication, when the panic attacks magically disappeared. I still do not know why I was put on an anti-psychotic for the treatment of anxiety. Doctors, in my experience, do not talk to or listen to their patient, they just dictate. Recently I had to persuade the doctors not to put me back on the medication that made me ill.

I believe that I would have dealt better with my mother's illness and have less problems myself, if right at the beginning I had been listened to and heard. I needed to be acknowledged as a person with their own needs and not ignored by the professionals.

Anon

Terry'99.

THE FORGOTTEN ONES

What no one ever seems to realize is that I am the forgotten one, hidden by a fake wall of happiness. I've been sitting behind this wall for quite a while now, and I am beginning to get cramp. If only I could stretch my legs, gather up my energy and peep over the wall. Then everybody would see me, get a glimpse at what I am really protecting behind this barrier. Maybe if I had enough courage I could jump over the wall, or even knock it down, maybe.

My mum has been a manic depressive all my life. That's where it all started, with me. When I was born, the post-natal depression started, but as I grew up the depression didn't go away. It reoccurred, and hounded my mother as manic depression. So I mothered my mother through her bad times, her ups and downs, her highs and lows. I have learned to be a good listener and councillor. I learned how to be a responsible adult before I learned to be a child, and that is my one regret. When I look back on my childhood, I remember how at the age of four I comforted my mother's sobs, kept the house clean at the age of seven and cooked the dinner at the age of twelve. My mum constantly tells me what a bad mother she has been to me. I just remind her of how well I have turned out, a responsible young adult. And it's true; it was all down to her, and her illness.

It's getting worse. It gets worse every time. Don't get me wrong, there have been good times, between the bad. But why is it that you always remember the bad times over the good? When I do remember a good time, it's like a little ray of sunshine, but then I realise that there are dark, heavy clouds rolling in from the left and right, above and below. Sometimes I wish that there was just a little bit more sunlight shining on me.

Anon

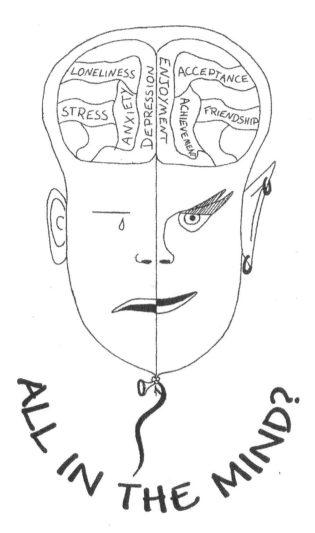

Illustration by Lewis Warner, from The Dove Centre, Chelmsford, Creative Writing Group's Book of Poems. The Dove Centre is now known as MIND.

The Dove Centre is no longer in Chelmsford

THROUGH THE EYES OF A CARER

People often ask me, as Margaret's husband, how do you put up with her depression and cope with it all? The easy way would be to walk out and leave her, even get divorced. I have been able to adapt and accept her illness as part of our married life. As I said nineteen years ago, "in sickness and in health." In this way, we as a couple can work together and make the most of it. After all, manic depression is an illness that is always there, it can only be suppressed with the help of drugs. I think I should be asking Margaret 'how do you cope with depression?' She cannot run away from it. Depression is with her almost all of the time - awake and asleep, twenty-four hours a day - so she has no choice but to accept the illness.

There are times when the depression does lift, the dark clouds go and the sun shines. These are the times to cherish, and to enjoy ourselves together.

However, then we think this is too good to be true, and you begin to wonder how long it will last until the depression sets in again.

As yet I have not mentioned Michelle, our dear daughter, who is now 17 years old. I can honestly say that having her has given me the strength to persevere and stand by my wife, to keep us all together as a family.

When asked how I cope with Margaret's highs, I say that I have to take the easy (or perhaps the only) way out and turn my back on her. There is no way that I can handle or cope with the situation, a case of having to be cruel to be kind. When she has these high times she, in her own mind, is right in all respects. Everybody else is wrong. I cannot even reason, or communicate, with her.

The only escape for me, and for our daughter, is to have her admitted to hospital. During these times I really feel I don't exist in her mind. In the early days of her illness she would manipulate me into thinking that I was the one who was at fault, and I would believe it. I must admit I was driven to despair, not realizing that her actions were all part of manic depression. The only good thing during these highs is knowing that eventually she will be home from hospital and our relationship will return one day to normality again. Now that Margaret finally accepts that she suffers from this problem, I know that one day we can leave this all behind us and look forward to a brighter future.

Stewart
1949-2004

4. CARERS:

4b Thoughts on Carers

MY HOME HELP

At one time when I was ill I was eligible for a home help. A lady called Barbara would come round once a week to help me with housework. She usually used to do the ironing for me whilst I did the washing (at this time I had a twin tub). The idea was for me to have help, not just in a practical way but also by talking to me in a therapeutic way. We became very good friends, even to a point where we would see each other socially, and my family were also invited to one of her daughter's weddings. I loved her dearly and was very upset to hear she had died from a tumour on the brain. I feel that I may suffer badly with my illness, but I get to know some wonderful people who really care and like to get involved with people like myself. I have been fortunate enough to get to know people who really care and want nothing more than to give so very much to people like myself. I will never forget Barbara.

Margaret

MY DAUGHTER MICHELLE AND I

My first experience of depression was post-natal depression. It seems such a long time ago now - nearly 18 years. I remember lacking confidence so much, and feeling I had this helpless bundle who cried and cried. I just felt as if I didn't have a clue as to what I should be doing. Everything seemed a mess - in my mind as well as the state of the house!

It took me quite a while to eventually feel better again - I don't remember how long exactly, but you do eventually get well again. Over the years I have suffered from depression, and it hasn't done any harm to my daughter, in fact I feel we are closer than a lot of mums and their offspring are. In some ways she feels it is an advantage as she has become totally sympathetic and compassionate towards people who do suffer in this way. We have a priceless relationship.

There were times when it was very difficult to cope with having my daughter, but, with God's help, I always got through somehow. Having a good relationship with my daughter has always been very important to me. I may not have achieved as much in life as I may have wanted, but bringing Michelle up was one vocation I wanted to get right. I'm sure there must have been times for her when she saw me going through some very bad patches, but I feel sure that at these times we grew stronger together. Most families experience their own problems, and sometimes they get through it and sometimes it breaks the family up. When this illness strikes, it puts a great deal of strain on my family, and we find ourselves near breaking point. For the last 17 years this illness has invaded our lives many times, and we are still together. Maybe as a family we do suffer at times, but I feel we have grown strong. I feel that if we can manager some how to cope with this illness, then we can survive *anything.* So in that respect we are truly blessed.

Margaret

5. FOOD:

5a Weight Watching

I wrote this in hospital where we were told that "food is not the issue", but where the programme was based on rewarding good weight gain with privileges, such as phone calls and visitors. For me, food was far from the only issue, but it was the most important one which I needed to deal with and I often felt that no-one really knew what to do with me to help deal with my other problems.

FOOD IS NOT THE ISSUE

Food is not the issue
At least that's what you said;
It's not underlying problems
And not just to be fed.

I opened up my heart
And I let you see inside;
The feelings and the thoughts
Can no longer be denied.

My life's in little pieces,
I thought that I would mend
And put it back together
Without having to pretend.

You said I would be safe here,
I knew I had to try,
But now you've gone and left me
And there's no more tears to cry.

I still feel the pain and terror
Which you cannot understand,
But it doesn't fit the programme
Which you've carefully planned.

I came in here, I trusted you,
I thought you'd make me well.
My body may be mended
But my soul has gone to hell.

3rd October 1996   Jacqueline Monger

I wrote this a few weeks after I left hospital, weighing a very uncomfortable and frightening 1.5 stones heavier that I'd ever been in my life, even when I was reasonably well. People saw me "looking better" on the outside, so assumed I was better on the inside too, which I wasn't.

<u>NOBODY KNOWS</u>

The smile on my lips says everything's fine,
The nightmare within rarely shows
And the pain in my soul that is hidden away
Is silent, so nobody knows.

My fears often have to stay buried,
My tears often now go un-cried,
But the body I see bears the marks of my pain
And the torment and hurting inside.

Yet I'm looking so well on the outside,
No longer so thin I appal,
So why when I ought to be better
Do I still feel the need to be small?

And I know that my body is fitter
If I eat what I should every day,
Yet the urge to be thin and unfed
Still remains and it won't go away.

And the mornings, they come too quickly
And the days are still such a fight;

I long for sleep to have some peace
But there's no escape at night.

The dark is no longer a friend of mine
When I close my eyes in bed;
When I feel so despairing and very alone
With the thoughts that are in my head.

So I switch on the light and the radio too
And fight off the panic that grows,
But the screaming inside me that comes from my soul
Is silent so nobody knows.

January 1997   Jacqueline Monger

6. DIAGNOSES AND WELFARE:

6a Benefits

BENEFITS

I feel something should be done to help people with mental health problems to obtain benefits. I have been a sufferer for 18 years, and only this year have I known about and been able to claim severe disablement benefit. I didn't know it existed until this year. I wouldn't have been able to cope with the forms on my own - this year a good friend's husband has helped me to fill in the forms. I have had encouragement to go for this benefit.

If you don't have any of the above support, then how do you stand any chance of claiming what you are entitled to? Mental Illness makes it impossible for many sufferers to claim for what they are entitled to. More help and awareness is needed.

Anon

6. DIAGNOSES AND WELFARE:

6b Care in the community

A SUCCESS STORY

It takes time and isn't easy
but I'm getting there
To become another success story
Of community care.

I am in the community
And not shut away
In some Victorian asylum
Till my dying day.

I live and work
To earn my daily bread
And have a mortgage
On the roof above my head.

I want to dispel the myth
And the public's views
That people with schizophrenia
Are all bad news.

Give us the time and resources
That we badly need
Then community care will work
And then, we might all succeed!

Jim Wilson

GOD KNOWS

Not so long ago
If a person fell prey
To a mental illness
They were shut away.

Now there is a change
As asylums in every town
In a few years' time
Will nearly all be shut down.

People who exist in hospitals
Will be found new places to live
This is called community care.
A new directive.

So people who used to exist
Out of mind, out of sight,
Will be in the community
To battle in their plight.

Many will need lots of help
For them to survive
But in mind I have no doubt
That some will thrive.

As history goes to show
An illness of the mind

Is linked to many geniuses
Of humankind.

And God knows we need a genius,
Who might be in an institution,
To sort out this insane world
Which needs a revolution!

Jim Wilson

6. DIAGNOSES AND WELFARE:

6c Day Care

Picture framing is one of the projects at Millrace, Chemsford.

SOLUTION FOCUS

The Day Hospital has groups running that are suitable for people at each stage of their recuperation. One of the groups I attended was for those who were on the mend. It was called 'Solution Focus'. There would be around five people who attended this group and two members of staff.

Each week, each person attending the group would fill out a form which asked questions about what they had experienced during their week. Those who had just joined the group would find it difficult to write about anything good or bad that they had experienced during the previous week. By talking about their week, it was possible to see positive things. Maybe their previous week was not too good, but by talking, the staff would delve into what that person had written and point out that there was something positive. Perhaps that person had enjoyed the walk they had to the shops, even though they had written that doing the shopping had been a traumatic experience. As the weeks went by, the staff would help us to look for these positive signs.

I am at present in the throes of leaving the group. I have found this group invaluable. I have grown to be able to see things in a different light. No matter how bad things are (and fortunately things are now going well for me), I have gradually learnt of a way to look at my situation and be able to pull out the good things, no matter how small, and over the weeks build up a clear picture of the progress I am making. Long live this group!

Margaret

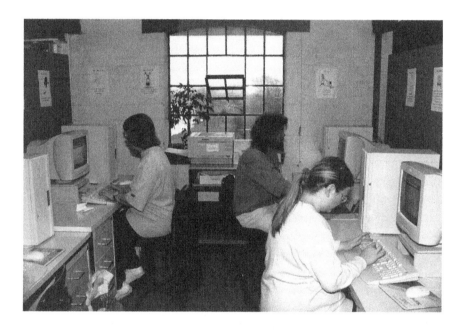

Millrace IT provides IT training to disadvantaged people.

The Mental Health Service. C & E Centre.

TAKE A BREAK

When my daughter was young I used to go to a coffee morning called 'Take-A-Break'. It was held at the Baptist Church in the town. They provided a crèche for the children. Each week we would do something different. A Social Worker was involved with the activities in the group. I used to look forward to going there. It was nice to have the children entertained while we mums had a break, and some kind of activity usually kept us busy. It was nice to build up friendships with the other mums who attended.

In the 'Cliff Richard Grapevine' magazine I receive there was an advertisement from a lady, called Margaret who had had a stroke and wanted people to write to her. Her name rang a bell. I wrote to her and asked if she used to help at Take-A-Break. It turned out to be Margaret, the same lady who used to help look after the children in the crèche. It was so good to be in touch with her via her carer, and nice to have a mutual interest in Cliff Richard.

Margaret

This was in the days of the Rainbow Clubhouse work scheme, Chelmsford.

This was The Rainbow Clubhouse

25/2/98

RAINBOW CLUBHOUSE

I have been attending the Rainbow Clubhouse for nearly a year now. It is a centre especially for people like me, with mental health problems. I enjoy going there very much. Everyone plays an important role. The Clubhouse is run jointly by the staff as well as the members (mental health sufferers). Nearly all the work which the staff do is also taught and done by the members. Members also have a say in who is employed at the Clubhouse. The work which is done there can be anything from working out statistics and answering the phone, to booking in people who wish to visit the centre. I personally have gained a great deal of confidence through attending the Clubhouse. As a direct result I find myself fulfilling an ambition of mine, which is what you are reading now. I have felt for quite some time that I would like to write a book about mental illness, but without the Clubhouse I think that it would all have been just a pipe dream. It is now a reality.

The staff are there to support us when the time comes that members are suffering from mental illness. At this time when you are feeling at your worst, you are allowed to take a back seat and take it easy by just sitting and drinking coffee, if that is all you feel up to doing. The welfare of members is always put first. It is wonderful belonging to Rainbow Clubhouse as you really feel you are being cared for. If you are distressed, the staff will spend time with you if you wish. They will reassure you and help to put how you are feeling into perspective.

Margaret

The Rainbow Clubhouse has since closed.

RAINBOW CLUBHOUSE

The Rainbow Clubhouse is a special place
Important, one and all are made to feel
We each have our special talents
The staff are there to help highlight
To make the most of what we have to offer
We each care for one another
We can be ourselves
In pain or in pleasure
We have a place to go
We are like a family
To be ourselves, we are accepted
We're home!

Margaret

The Rainbow Clubhouse has since closed.

This is the Dove Centre (now known as MIND) when it was in
Broomfield Road. July 1995 - 2001

The Dove Centre is no longer in Chelmsford.

CHELMSFORD AND DISTRICT MIND
(FORMALLY KNOWN AS THE DOVE CENTRE)

I have been going to Chelmsford and District MIND since around 1982. At present I attend the 'Women's Group' on a Tuesday morning, the 'Creative Writing Group' on a Thursday morning and 'Drop in' on a Thursday afternoon.

The Women's Group You are free to come and go. There is a good atmosphere and plenty to talk about. Afterwards, it is off to a venue for a drink and a meal if you wish.

Creative Writing Group is a time to get the brain working! We are given a different subject to write about each week - or we can write about anything we would like to.

Drop In is as it suggests, a time for members to 'drop in', to come and have a coffee and a chat. It is a good time to meet other members, volunteers and staff.

Margaret

The Dove Centre is now closed.

The Chelmsford Women's Group meeting on a Tuesday morning
at The Dove Centre that is now known as MIND.

The Dove Centre is no longer in Chelmsford.

MHAG - MENTAL HEALTH ACTION GROUP

When the burden of your heart
Bears upon itself once more
Remember that
There's a place in town
For your worries and your frown.
It's called MHAG

Ralph Marshall

Interact aims to help others help themselves, working with people who have mental health problems and young people with learning disabilities.

DROP-INS

I have schizophrenia
And when I feel low
There are certain places
Where I can go.

They are drop-in centres
In the middle of town.
They are ideal places
When I feel down.

I have a cup of tea,
Chat with members and staff,
I get troubles off my mind
And sometimes even laugh.

Then when I leave
I find my mood has shifted,
I don't feel so depressed
And often feel uplifted!

Jim Wilson

<u>MIND HOW YOU GO</u>

I used to sit at home on my own,
In my illness I felt all alone.
I would take a walk around the streets
No one would I want to meet.

After hospital care I still felt alone.
Then the helpers of Maldon MIND Group came along,
We meet in Tillingham once a week
To go there and talk is such a treat.

Go swimming and have lunches, it gets us all out,
And nobody worries what we are talking about.
It does not cost a penny to go to the hall,
The fare is free; a car takes us all.

So do not worry if you are not feeling well,
Or if you have a hurtful story to tell.
Come to Maldon MIND, they will make you feel good.
You will feel happier and stronger just as you should.

Jean

MIND LUNCH ON A RAINY DAY

We all met at the Bradwell King's Head,
About the wet weather nothing was said.
We had huge lunches that filled every plate,
In spite of all the food, all the lot we ate.

My daughter was visiting me at the time,
And for her to come with us made the day just fine.
We sat for a while to have a talk,
Then out in the rain we had to walk.

By the car park was a field that belonged to the pub,
In the field were two pet llamas and in the rain they stood.
As Peggy stood below her brolly to keep her from the rain,
A llama came and grabbed it and we laughed until in pain.

Still laughing we all got in the cars,
We felt as though we had been through the wars.
The day had been such jolly good fun.
When home out of the rain we all had to come.

Jean Lomas

WHAT OF LIFE'S MAJESTIC EXISTENCE
MHAG - Mental Health Action Group

What of life's majestic existence?
Manifests itself to us
Beauty and the inland boundaries
Many lost and only a few.

When the burden of your heart
Bears upon itself once more
Remember that
There's a place in town
For your worries and your frown
It's called MHAG

Ralph

6. DIAGNOSES AND WELFARE:

6d Hospital

This is the Chelmsford Linden Centre for people with mental illnesses.

HIGH

As I become high, I become assertive and confident. I change from being boring old Mum and I feel I become the person I really am, but no one likes it. They become hostile and I become to feel angry and frustrated. I end up in hospital, they give you tablets to bring you down - when you are 'down' you come out of hospital and spend six months fighting depression! Anyway, that's how it used to be. I've got a super Doctor now - he really knows his stuff. Everybody hates you being different when you're high. They start making you feel alien. They are patronizing. Nothing gets sorted out because they say, "Oh, are you sure it's not just because of your illness?" You never get anywhere. When you're in hospital, they tell you to make the decision when you're well, when you're normal. What's normal? When am I ever normal? Over the last two years I've either been high as a kite or flat as a pancake. So when do I get to sort out my life?

Anon

MY EXPERIENCE

Unless you have experienced any kind of mental health problem, it is hard to consider that it could easily happen to anyone, at any time in any walk of life. My first encounter was when I was 23 years old. I am now 36 years old and am pleased to say that the treatment I have received in the not too long forgotten past has been much appreciated.

The support at the Linden Centre from the staff, doctors and the consultant, and the way my case was dealt with, has been quite remarkable compared to my stay at Severalls all those years ago. I have mixed memories of the things that happened then, some good, some bad. The good feeling is the togetherness of people in some kind of strife. I felt this for the first time at Severalls, and remember a lot of the nurses with great admiration. A not so great experience that I remember was being shipped out in a mini bus for E.C.T. A plump Japanese nurse called out our names as we were driven off to our fates. I can remember her saying my name (then Barber). She called me 'Babba' in her accent, and it sent a chill down my spine, like something awful was about to happen. Needless to say I have survived.

I think the stigma is gradually being erased, but a lot more needs to be done to make people today realise that suffering from mental health does not make a person an alien to the rest of the world, but often a more caring and thoughtful, self-critical person whose needs, like everyone's, are of the greatest importance.

I have experienced the greatest support from the other people who were patients at the Linden Centre in August/September

1997, and my family and friends, not forgetting my husband and son.

Some people are not as fortunate as I have been, and that is why everyone should be able to be given the opportunity to believe in the mental health care of today and the future.

Jean

I REMEMBER YOU

I remember you,
Sharing a room with you.
You brought me tea in the mornings.
I thought what a kind girl you were.

I remember you
Now that you are gone
Gone to a place
Where you can now feel that love,
The love you were so desperate for.

I remember you,
Your Mum came to visit.
She'd stay and talk.
I left you alone together.

I remember you now
A bright sparkling girl
Full of love and care for the world.
I remember you Jayne.
You were a friend for a short time
    to me.

                                        Jean

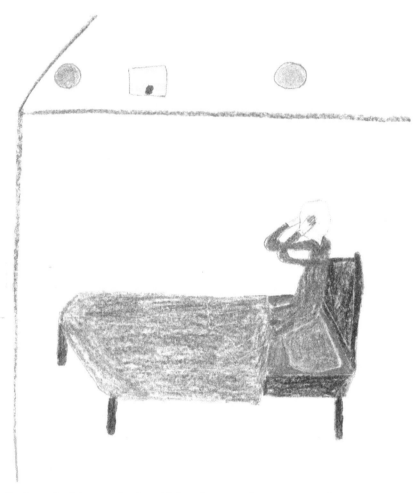

In hospital it can feel as if they're watching you in the privacy of
your own room.

CLANKING PIPES

When I was in hospital in 1997 I was very mistrusting. I looked at the spotlight in the ceiling and was convinced there was a camera up there watching me, not a light. I moved the bed in my room so I was away from the 'light'. I was later moved to another room where the pipes rattled. I felt convinced that they had put me in a room that really was a gas chamber. Every now and again I would go for a walk for some fresh air. I wondered what else it could have possibly been: clanking pipes in the summer?

Margaret

ANDREW

During the day, the trolleys come and go
Tea, lunch, supper, medication and, at night, cocoa.
The nurses watch and tip the wink,
To the doctor, when they think
You're not as well today as you were yesterday
And could definitely do with a longer stay.

What shall we do today? The morning screams through the
window.
Shall we sit and read the newspaper to let the world knows
You're just a regular person aware of world events
Or read it upside down so they may get a sense
Of how much you distrust their little game
Implying that getting to know you should be their aim.

Sometimes he sits and stares along the corridor
The strange and the familiar seem more
Or less oblivious to his observant presence there.
What is the prognosis for the illness where
Neither kind and unkind, the wicked and the good
Know what to do or would do it if they could?

Looking for a bath plug in hospital - those were the days!

EASTLAKE WARD

The long blue corridor of Eastlake Ward and beyond that, at the far end, the way downstairs to the day area, to other wards and to the outside world.

Shapes would materialise behind those double doors during the day, a visitor, another patient, a cleaner, the food trolley and more important, in terms of interrupting the routine, that the latter, would be a doctor, possibly arriving Kafkaesque, to make some decision about one's case. The smell from the animal laboratories as one walked round the perimeter. The words like 'section', the locked doors, the chemical hazard signs, 'perimeter', the keys carried by the nurses, all that mystique of Russian psychiatry, fuelled the illusion that this was something to do with the intelligence services, that there was something political about it.

The mysterious process of getting better, when the delusions left you, and you were left with the emptiness of nothing to do, and the gnawing restlessness in the body caused by drugs.

The simplicity of physical illness by comparison: he remembered his allergic reaction to largactil when his face swelled up to the size of a football, and the obvious sympathy and kindness that this elicited from the nurses.

The belief that he could communicate almost telepathically with old women from Elder Ward in the canteen, the older and wiser women, as if they had something in common against the more simplistic people around them. How they were all exceptional to the utmost extreme, in some way or other, archetypes of intelligence, wisdom or class.

Throwing a large softball from one to another in a circle in the Common Room. The pianos, which did not tune, the tape machines, record players and radio which didn't play; the one sided table-tennis bats, the cracked table tennis balls.

They used to take away your clothes when you arrived in the early days, and a sure sign that you were getting better was having them returned to you. Then being allowed down to the shop accompanied by a nurse, then to the downstairs canteen, then to walk around the grounds of the hospital, then home leave, and out: a kind of geographical progress that accompanied one's getting better, and which was easier to understand.

The board games with missing pieces, the 49 pack of cards, the dirty toilets, all the victims of public use and which seemed to reflect one's battered and run-down situation.

The unreality of the shop, the library, the public telephones, the nurses' 'office' - seeming to be things of the world outside, but robbed of their normality by the veneer of abnormality cast over them by the hospital surroundings.

Phoning the G.P. on his first night in hospital to assure him that he was quite well and didn't need to be in here; asking to be let out.

He taught the girl to do press-ups because he thought this would help with her condition. He later saw her working on the perfume counter in Harrow, and thought how misguided his suggested therapy had been.

"And how are we feeling today Mr. Watkiss?" Doctor asked. The use of the conjunction made him feel that his condition was complementary to, or, probably more likely, intrusive upon, some other set of circumstances circumambient upon the Doctor rather than himself, while the direct concern for himself that the question ostensibly offered was further eroded by the flexible embrace of the pronoun from this patient, to this interlocutory pair, to the patients on the ward generally.

His fantasy diminished the importance of the question anyway, to a mere introductory gambit in a wider game: the game of preparing him to be head of British Secret Intelligence. For this was his fantasy, or so the doctors would have called it had he been able to reveal it to them, and this was his reality, for most of the time. All crucial decisions for the benefit of his life could be analysed in terms of the British Intelligence Service and his potential role as its head. It was a simple matter to make the ward a 'cell'; the computers and medicine, mind controlling equipment, and the doctors KGB agents who had infiltrated MI6.

This delusion was part of a state of mind, which he later learned was called 'paranoid schizophrenia', the full-blown variety. A gargantuan name for a gargantuan condition. People often asked him if he was aware that his delusions were a fantasy. . The answer to the question was an emphatic no. They were, could only be, although varying in degree of incipience, reality. That was why he was mad; the delusions were a commitment, and he didn't stand apart from himself and look down to see what was absurd. The absurd was all there was, and it therefore ceased to be absurd.

When the doctor went on to ask him if he had had any strange thoughts his answer was, unhesitatingly, "no." And anyway, the very surroundings lent a logic to the fantasy; the grey institutional decor, the hospital's lack of commercialism, the perimeter fence, the colourless facades against which certain coloured objects – motor vehicles, pills, emergency alarms - became 'special' objects. He has since come to sympathise with this question. How else could he put it, anyway? 'Any delusions?' was too pejorative; 'any difficulty with your thinking?' was also vaguely insulting. Once a nurse had described his thinking as too 'tangential' for him to be able to leave the hospital, suggesting that it didn't follow a logical sequence. His thoughts were indeed 'passing strange'.

The doctor was a tall woman who perched on an adjustable stool, adjusted so that her feet only just touched the floor. This fact, combined with the fact that he was deemed to be mad, out of control, in need of care, emphasised the imbalance in their relationship. To him, it was an important relationship, for the doctor held the key to his freedom. To have an appointment to see the doctor made one the envy of the ward.

The interview could offer the possibility of a decision, of progress; of information about one's case, what the doctors thought of you, and what they thought of doing with you. It offered a potential attention to one's predicament. Something definite. From this point of view, he accepted the imbalance.

The simple answer to the doctor's question about 'strange thoughts' was simply, "no", which was honest to the extent that to him the delusions were only fact, but economical with the truth to the extent that he had more than a slight suspicion that something pretty serious had brought him in here, and that that something had to do with 'strange thoughts'.

"But I get a lot of restlessness, I can't relax" he added. "That'll be the drug," the doctor confirmed. He knew. The patients called it the 'medicate shuffle'. You watched them waiting, sitting in the chairs downstairs for the restaurant to open, legs twitching up and down as if in time to some silent demonic music. You couldn't keep still, and even when the dance was absent, you had a feeling of tension throughout the body. A subtle form of torture, and made worse because it was difficult to describe and, in most cases, not physically apparent. The doctor took his arm and bent it to the elbow. "Are you taking the procycladine?" "Yes," he replied. "I think we might increase that."

The suggestion did not encourage him. The sole purpose of the interview as far as he was concerned was to convince the doctor of his return to normality, to reduce the medication into his body, and be assured of his imminent release. An increase in medication did not fall within this, did not fall within this scheme. Worse was to follow. "The nurses tell me you're often up and about late at night. Why is that?" It was partly, of course, because he couldn't sleep, but it had more to do with the fact that the circumscribed unreality of the night reflected very well with his own condition; the narrowing of the world into a confined private place, the special quality of existence that being aware in the night had. That special quality reflected well his own disturbed state.

"I find it hard to sleep and I like the atmosphere on the ward at night." "Would you like me to prescribe you some sleeping pills?" "No, it's all right," he replied. The suggestion had gone right against what he hoped would be the direction of the consultation: reduction in the medication and reduction of time compelled him to stay in hospital. "On the whole we're very pleased with you. We think you've made a lot of progress since you've been here." This was the opener to the crucial question to which every consultation led, the 'how long will I have to be in here question', if he had the courage to ask it, fearing the reply..........

Anon

ANDREW

He sat in his favourite chair looking down the long ward to the doors at the end. The doors were rarely locked: this was an 'acute' ward, which was not, as its name suggests a place for the most seriously ill. The most serious cases would distinguish you from day patients who came and went as they pleased, and you were under observation; you might be a 'voluntary' patient, or you might have been admitted by your G.P., or worse than this you might have been 'sectioned', for three days, twenty-eight days or six months. A sectioned patient was considered 'a danger to himself and others' or, at best, a potential danger. Such a patient lost the right to come and go as he pleased. Some years ago this denial would be exercised at the onset of one's stay in hospital by the removal of one's clothes and their replacement by pyjamas and dressing gown, though one would keep one's shoes. For one's clothes to be unlocked from the ward cupboard and returned to them was a sign that one was getting better.

So the people he saw coming and going from dormitories to the left of the corridor were all categorised in different ways. They all had different staff; some voluntary, some sectioned, some there for schizophrenia, some for depression, some getting better, some getting worse, some who had been there days, some months, some who had been there or in similar places many times, some never before, some compliant and taking their medication, some refusing it, some quiet, some rowdy, some who appeared quite sane, others who were quite obviously not well. But I suppose what they all had in common was their unpredictability. This is what a 'section' was all about: you might have done nothing wrong, dangerous or anti-social, but nobody could predict that you wouldn't. People couldn't rely on you, and the purpose of the drugs was, if nothing else, to make you more predictable; that, after all, has a lot to do with the purpose of science: It had to do with predicting how things would behave, establishing laws.

There was then a contradiction: the purpose of the treatment was to make you reliable and predictable: the purpose of the illness, if it could be said to have one, was to make you unreliable and unpredictable. It seemed scarcely credible that this contradiction could be resolved by a dose of tablets taken two or three times a day.

The rattle of keys as a nurse left the 'office' and headed for the medicine room heralded medication time. This did not fill him with apprehension today, for he had recently fallen for what seemed to him the pristine logic of a nurse's advice that a day now meant an extra day at the end, meaning that a delay in taking medication would result in a longer stay. He would have been apprehensive if he had decided not to heed this advice, and an altercation at the medicine trolley would have ensued during which he would refuse the medication and the nurse would indicate by subtle expression or gesture that this would be all the worse for him, not simply because he would not get better, but he would remain in what people generally regarded as an unregenerate state. It was almost a sin not to take medication in this place, which was entirely dedicated to making one well.

Why didn't he want to take the medication previously? Willingness so to do presupposes the ability to distinguish between health and illness. To accept himself as ill was rather different from accepting that one had a cold. He was not sick in body and mind, degenerate, almost evil. The sickness pervaded his whole being like a possession. He was not to be reasoned with yet he was to be pitied. To accept the illness was to accept a kind of condemnation.

The last thing he wanted to do was to accept that he was ill; his illness, his way of looking at things, the illness seen from the inside, if you like, was really all he had to cling to. Nothing else had any value. To accept the medication was to accept that somebody somewhere knew better. These drugs, manufactured in the laboratory and administered by those who were not completely sure how they worked, or even if they worked, or even if they would work, seemed a poor substitute for sympathy or the power of language, which he felt were the two methods that should have been employed to treat this mental, physical and emotional aberration that was illness. It took so many forms, had so many expressions in different people, and in the same person, so how could a single cocktail of chemicals treat so many different symptoms? Where was the art of being a doctor prescribing, what seemed in many cases, to be simply a placebo?

But now, having admired the simple logic of the nurse's words (not their practical truth, that he would get out earlier), he downed the little white nonentities with the small plastic beaker of water provided and returned to his watching and listening post. The medication trolley was wheeled away, and the next major event of the day was the approach of another trolley, mid-morning coffee, then a still larger trolley, lunch, the medication trolley again, afternoon-tea, supper, the medication trolley and finally the cocoa-trolley at 10 p.m. These events were actually laid out on a timetable on the wall of the ward, with nothing between them. And there was nothing between them. Life glided on this irksome routine like astronauts inside their space shuttle, protected from the outside of their craft, burning at millions of degrees, flames leaping across the cockpit windows, as they re-entered the earth's atmosphere. The illness was like the outside of the spacecraft, the ostensible life, like the inside, weightless and unreal.

So what would the day bring, between the coming and going of trolleys? The ultimate disruption would be the arrival of a doctor on the ward, possibly with news of one's case. The doctor had great power; he could determine whether one was getting better or worse. He could predict how long one would have to remain here. Things could be going along quite normally when a patient could be told out of the blue that he could have his clothes back, or he could leave the ward to visit the shop, take a walk, or even have weekend leave. One would have noticed no discernible change in this person's behaviour and yet somewhere, somehow, a decision had been made which entirely changed the prognosis. For this reason, the arrival of a doctor was felt, by all the patients, to be an event of singular importance. To be interviewed by one was probably the most sought-after event. Then could one get some idea of the progress of one's illness and the likely length of stay. This was a subject he never liked to broach in such interviews for fear of disappointment, so the key question often remained unanswered. Only if the doctor volunteered an opinion as to, for instance, allowing one to walk in the hospital grounds, did one feel they were getting anywhere. Everyone had one aim in life: to leave hospital. All endeavours were narrowed to this one intent.

Even to reach the stage of being able to ask this question was an advantage, for it was always preceded by other questions at earlier points in one's stay. When will I get my clothes back? When will I be allowed out for a walk? When will I be able to eat downstairs (as opposed to on the ward)? To achieve these stages of rehabilitation was progress indeed. And now one was at the apex of opportunity with the question: when will I get out?

Looking back this question seemed to have symbolic import. The ward as a microcosm of the universe. Pumped full of drugs, one's destiny not one's own, either in one's ability to control one's thoughts and desires, or the ability of other people and the world

at large to control them for you. When will I get out? The eschato-
logical approach to life.

What were the rudiments of life on the ward, the tools available
to one to make an 'escape'? A chair, a table, regular food, and func-
tionaries whose interest, or at least understanding, of you was best
tangential and superficial. Other patients who sometimes seemed
to be in a worse situation than you, frankly beyond the pale, or
who, because of some unannounced knowledge, were in a privi-
leged position, particularly as regards 'getting out'. Not so different from normal life.......

THE IN-PATIENT
The Linden Centre

I remember in 1996 I was very high and in hospital. When I am high I just am not the Margaret Mitchell I know when I am well. My behaviour changes. I go along with a whim of my over inflated behaviour believing I am right about everything and that 'they' are the enemies. I am on my guard waiting for 'them' to do wrong by me. 'They' tend to be my family and staff; I feel friends are on 'my side' (or can be influenced to be on my side). With family and staff, I really feel I have to watch my back. I really have a personality change and are really offhanded and aggressive with them. I'm just not me. I remember Stewart, my husband, coming to see me, and I would send him off home again because he had bought me the wrong brand of cola and crisps. I had so much condemnation for them all. Even thinking I should divorce this awful man (that poor old beloved husband of mine). I remember going round and crossing out all of the Fire Exit signs on the doors and changing the smoking room to the lounge. I was experiencing all sorts of out-of-character behaviour. I think deep down I was just so petrified, I just couldn't trust anyone, so much so that I didn't sleep for three or four days. I was too frightened of what might happen if 'they' had the chance. But at least I had my Cliff Richard's CDs and cassettes, so Cliff helped me as I felt he was a friend - even though it drove everyone up the wall by my constant repeat playing! I listened to him nearly all the time.

It was an awful time for me, as I felt very much alone. When I do turn the corner and am able to trust people once again it feels good, but that also means I go from being very high to going low.

Although that is very much easier for everyone to cope with, it also means a long, slow progression to eventually feeling 'normal' again.

Margaret

SPECIAL CARE UNIT

When I was ill and staying in The Linden Centre, I guess my behaviour must have been a cause for concern, as I ended up in the Special Care Unit. This was quite a frightening experience as you were put in there for your own good, and, if necessary, forcibly placed in there. The special care unit consisted of a small lounge, with a telly which was covered with a protective plastic layer, a couple of bedrooms, a toilet and a shower. There were a couple of staff within the unit who kept you there until they felt you were beginning to behave in a more 'normal' manner. I was very frightened, as I wasn't well and did not understand what was happening. One time when I was in there turned out to be my turning point. I felt as if I was being locked away and would not ever escape. Maybe I would never see my relatives or friends ever again. Eventually, when my husband did come and visit me in there, I realized just how much I loved and needed him. I am sure that was my turning point in my illness. It felt as though I had been abandoned for good, and all of a sudden my husband appeared like a knight in shining armour. He had come and saved me. I believe in this kind of illness there is a turning point that you reach, as though you are going through a muddled tunnel of turmoil and then all of a sudden you see a light, which grows until you start to come back in touch with reality again.

Margaret

GRIP OF MANIC DEPRESSION

This piece was written when I was in _the grip of Manic Depression_. I think I must have been feeling 'high'.

When you're in hospital, they make you sleep. When you wake, you eat, sleep and receive 'therapy'. It's great fun, you get three meals provided and you can behave as silly as you like while you're in there. You can have a second childhood. After all, they expect it of you, and you wouldn't want to disappoint them would you?

Leading up to your admission, you become really interested in what you have become involved with. So you become more active as you are enjoying it, more confident. I was once taught assertiveness skills, which these days have proved very useful. But at that time, because I did change, people did not respond well, I had changed, I was keeping busy. "Crumbs, watch out, she'll be back in hospital acting like that." So I felt everything I did was scrutinized. It becomes annoying. I am not a child. All those closest to you become angry and authoritative. The ones you need most for support can't cope, yet it is me who ends up in hospital. When you need those closest to you to be there for you they turn against you. You are alone. Still, at least you have three free meals provided and you have washing done for you by your 'caring' relations.

Nobody ever seems to be able to find out what is at the root of the problem. They never take that much notice of what you tell them. It is really odd; if you have a broken leg there is an awful amount of fuss made: x-rays, location of pain, nice nurse popping in regularly to tuck you in. It's not like that for people like me. I remember once they asked what I did, and so I told them that I was a brain surgeon.

They hardly spent any time with you, though one nurse did, but she was having a break from working and having a cigarette, which I believe she shouldn't have done. So they take their breaks from work to sit with the patient, and she gets back to work doing her paperwork, such is the life of a caring sharing psychiatric nurse. Least if she gave stamps it would be a beneficial process.

Anon

WILL I EVER BE FREE?

I wrote this when I was in hospital and finding therapy difficult and wasn't sure if the staff really knew how I was feeling.

Will I ever be free
Of the pain inside?
Will I ever feel safe
Without needing to hide?

Will I ever be happy
When I'm feeling so sad?
Do I want to live
When I'm feeling so bad?

When I smile do you think
That I'm really OK,
When I'm crying inside
And I can't even say?

Will I ever be free
From the thoughts in my head?
And the pictures I see
Make me wish I was dead.

Will I see his face
Or say his name
Without tearing apart
And dying of shame?

Can I speak the words
That I need to say?
Can I make them real
Without running away?

When I'm feeling so desperate
That I can't even cry,
When I feel so alone
Then I wish I could die.

Will I ever get out
Of this great black hole?
Will somebody please
Help to mend my soul?

21st October 1996   Jacqueline Monger

6. DIAGNOSES AND WELFARE:

6e Medication

TEAM WORK

My psychiatrist is a very professional man
Who tries to help me as much as he can.
Every few months we meet and have a 'blether'
And both try hard to work together.
I used to take three drugs and be quite dopey,
I often felt fragile and my thoughts were ropy.
Now I only regularly take one new kind
Which helps to hone the thoughts in my mind.
My doctor has given me much insight,
Now I'm getting on fine and doing alright.
I have overcome much suffering and strife,
Now I have an appetite for and relish life.
By working together we have achieved success,
Now in my life I have found some happiness!

Jim Wilson

MEDICAL EXPECTATIONS

How can we talk, if we don't know how to communicate?
How can we be assertive, if we have not been taught?
How can facts be right, if assumptions are more important?
How can we be taken seriously, if we are patronized?
How can we give reasons, if they are turned into excuses?
How can we?

How can we co-operate, if there is no co-operation?
How can we be touched, if no one will reach?
How can we be calm, if we feel so much anger and frustration?
How can we shed our shell, when it's not safe to come out?
How can we finish, if we cannot start?
How can we?

How can we take the blame? Is it our fault?

How can we be intelligent,
         If we are treated as if we're not very bright?
How can black be white, if we know it's really black?
How can we change, if it ends up not being us?
How can people expect so much, when they give so little?
How can we have any rights, if we're not taken seriously?
How can I be me, if you can only see my disguise?
How can we?

How can we fill the void, when we've been given no fuel?
How can we be leaders, if we're just made to follow?

How can we find justice, when no-one wants the truth?
How can we ask, if it makes no difference?
How can we get there, if the journeys made too hard?
How can we?

How can we take the blame, is it our fault?

How can I think, when I'm so confused?
How can I give up hope?
       Sometimes it's the only thing to hold on to.
How can I give up faith? There is something to believe in.
How can I give up love? There is someone who loves us.

Margaret

DRUG MEDITATIONS

Older anti-psychotic drugs
Are relatively inexpensive
And their use in the treatment of schizophrenia
Is still very extensive.

There are newer anti-psychotics,
Drug companies are trying to sell,
Which have less side effects
And work just as well.

I would go as far as to say,
The new drug I take works better than that
As unlike the older ones
It doesn't leave me emotionally flat.

I now sometimes feel pleasure
And not just emotional pain
Due to the new chemicals
Carousing about my brain.

I now feel more alert
And not so doped and dozy
And think the future of the new drug
Looks altogether rosy.

So even though the new drug
Cost about sixty times as much

In reality I feel a hundred times
More in touch!

Jim Wilson

TRY UNDERSTANDING

I will start at the beginning. This will give a history of where things went wrong for me, showing the possibility that your early life can influence the way mental illnesses are created. Everyone is unique and the causes are different for every user or survivor, if there was a standard to go by, then life would be made easier, a "cure" maybe.

My experiences relate to my early life. At home, up to about eight, nine years of age, I was taught by my elder brother and father that you had to be aggressive or tough in life to earn respect. I felt as if I was kept on a lead, like a pet dog, and I was taught to use my aggression to hit other people or children. It did not matter how old or big the children were, and I did not need provocation or reason to fight. I was rewarded like a dog. My reward was affection, which was not shown except when I 'earned' it through my actions.

The only snag with having such a life is that you hide what you are actually like inside yourself, I was very artistic (I won my first art competition at the age of seven). I enjoyed nature, reading, poetry, etc. So I was living a double life, hiding the sensitive side to my nature, because I would not earn "rewards" for showing this.

Then at about twelve or thirteen, I had my first experience of depression. I became anti-social, totally against the system. I was dropped a class in school, from the 'A' class to the 'B' class, because of my lack of interest in school, which to them was a lack of intelligence. The school didn't know that my father had lost his job, my brother had left home to join the army, my sister had got married and left home, and my dog had died. Everybody I knew of my own age group was frightened of me, so they weren't really friends. It was not really talked about in the early sixties, and my parents did not tell the school anything that was going on. My local G.P. put me on Purple Hearts to calm me down: not exactly the ideal answer, but child psychologists were very few on the ground in those days, nobody wanted to know about mental illness. It was hidden away and not talked about.

At about the same time I was sexually assaulted by a local farmer. Again, everything was kept quiet and not talked about. Even the local police didn't want to know.

I joined art college direct from school, and had to leave six months later because of family financial problems. So I went back to the doctor's and was put on some kind of tablets. I was told "Don't worry, you will be alright, just take the tablets." I was not even told I was in a depressive state or suffering from an illness.

At about nineteen or twenty, I had my first schizophrenic experience. I kept on thinking someone was trying to suffocate me when I was sleeping. I could not sleep because I was afraid I would leave my body. I was hallucinating about the visitations of little men who kept telling me to beware I was an alien and I should go back to their planet. They probably call it a U.F.O. experience today. I find it quite comical really, today. I wonder if they are schizophrenic or if they have really experienced something. About the same time, I was sleepwalking to the extent that I was even taking a shower when I was asleep.

Although through my life I have had various incidents and various "visitors" in my brain (Do I have one?), and been treated by psychiatrists, psychologists, psychotherapy etcetera etcetera, it is very rare that any have told me exactly what is wrong with me. On one occasion I was threatened with E.C.T. to get me away from the psychiatrist, who was a trainee (a doctor on a six-month stint as a psychiatrist). The consultant told him this was not the right action. This affected me, and I thought all sorts of things. I went around shouting at people at every occasion, talking to myself, enjoying watching people's reactions to this as they didn't know where to put their faces in embarrassment. The other nice little trick I did was to bash my head on bus stops, signs and so on. Again the little people were telling me to do this; I was their agent.

This was when I was put in hospital for assessment and diagnosed as having schizophrenia. This was in Germany, and the doctors there put me on some tablets, one of which blew my head off and made me sleep, but they weren't too bad and pretty easy to use; the ones with a green band on them were for day time, the ones with the red band for night time. I was let out after two weeks, and visited the psychiatrist about every two weeks for about six months. The psychiatrist had the time to do counselling at the same time so I got 'better'.

I returned to England, but because my medical records were in Germany they refused to issue me with the necessary drugs that stabilised me, even though I told them about my illness. Approximately six months later I was told I was having a breakdown, which they again diagnosed as schizophrenia. So I was issued with the appropriate tablets yet again.

Why is it so hard to get doctors or psychiatrists to believe you? Why do they seem to 'guess' and use us as guinea pigs for drugs? Why do they never tell you exactly what's wrong with you until you ask? Why do they never tell you about other services or organisations you can use for your benefit? Are they frightened of losing control, frightened of disempowerment, scared of user-led organisations? I ask how many times do you go out to a user group and actually find a so-called 'professional' who is even interested in taking part, just to find what is happening on the 'other side'. Unfortunately, it is really still 'Us and Them' to a great extent.

Society has labelled me to fit in the slot provided by them, and when I admit to my mental illness I find a lot of people patronise me. It is mainly because of misunderstanding or believing in the media's negative portrayals of mental illness. I am waiting for the day when the media turn around and report all the good we can do. This would at least give a fairer picture of us.

In Greenwich (borough) where I live, the Mental Health Team of Social Services provide you with addresses of various organisations for users and survivors. The Health Authority do not give you any information about groups, just the usual odd leaflets in the waiting rooms. They have yet to come to the conclusion that user groups are great self-help groups as well. The best advocates are users themselves, and when we have been in the system quite a while we literally only need the doctors to prescribe our medication. I think once you get more confident about your illness the easier it is to handle. Initially you get guilt trips. "I can, I admit," seems only to come into the brain later on. The initial response is so despondent and you think, "I have a badge on top of my head, telling everyone that I am crazy. Oh my God, what will people think?"

I could carry on indefinitely over the subject of mental illness, but I will close with one small incident which happened to me last week.

I was told by Social Security that I was no longer entitled to income support/incapacity benefit because I did not attend the all work examination with one of their doctors. The reason I did not attend is because I never actually received a letter or form from them. So, after letters going backwards and forwards, I eventually went to the social security office. They said that I had been classed as capable of work. I said that that was strange, and that my G.P. and psychiatrist had just given me another thirteen weeks' sick note. They said to me "It doesn't matter about that now that we have classed you as capable of work." It appears now that the social security offices can decide if you are well or not. This is without medical opinions, without being assessed by a doctor at all. I went to the Law Centre here in Abbey Wood, who sorted it out for me. Apparently they are supposed to send you the examination form or whatever it is by recorded post, and if you do not attend they are supposed to follow up with a house visit. This rule applies to all mental illness sufferers. I have never known them move so fast. The law Centre appealed on my behalf over the phone and it was accepted there and then. I am now back on full benefits.

The reason I quote this from Social Security is that I found it very distressing and it put me on a "down". If this had happened a few years ago it would have made me suicidal, I am positive about that. It was proof to me the stigma still exists with certain people. They still have the attitude that mental illness sufferers don't need full explanations of the reasons behind their decisions. Why are we treated at times like second class citizens when we are normal people with sensitive feelings and needs?

Robert Hughes.

SURVIVAL

I had mild schizophrenic breakdown when I was in my forties - some ten years ago. I had periods of 'unsteadiness' for a few years previously when I lost weight and felt that things generally were slipping away from me. I was also, and am to a lesser degree these days, a carer as I have two sons who suffer from the condition. Thankfully at present, the three of us are stable and able to continue living our lives.

I wrote the following piece while I was ill which might convey some of the vulnerability that I felt.

> The yellowed surface of an ancient map
> Outlines diffused, squandered
> Flung out to the wind
> A game of chance
>
> Outstretched hands
> With gaunt fingers
> Of a transparent hue
> Reach out to touch
> The forgotten shapes

The clearest memory that I have is that of subjectivity. I was dominated by childhood experiences. My moods would swing. One minute I would laugh, which would become exaggerated only to be closely followed by tremendous sadness and weeping. I had to leave my centre.

When I was a carer I was on a low daily dosage of sulpiride and found some solace in evening drinking. I was sufficiently stable to live through the trauma each day. It was very difficult and not helped because the majority of people, including my extended family, did not want to recognise the problem - or so it seemed to me! People would relate to me their own problems and those of others. The general idea was to recognise that there were others far worse off than myself. In fact it had the opposite effect, I wrote this piece at that time - an attempt at expressing what I felt was the perversity of life:

> The wall is painted white
> It leaves no imprint of previous life
> The whiteness has absorbed all emotion
> It stands cold and clear
> Covering the dark stain
> That smashed its surface and
> Ran in rivulets to a conclusion

I hope maybe I have given you some help and wish you well with your book. People in similar situation to myself appreciate the support that you give.

Margaret R

THE RANGE AND SEVERITY OF VOICES

I have often been at odds with the doctors about the pointers to the severity of my illness, such as - which features suggest I am well and which suggest I am ill. The usual approach when I am hearing voices is to discover what the content of the voices is (what they are saying) and for what part of the day they are saying it. The content of the voices may be a useful clue to delusions and the abuse/control level may say something about the severity of the experience, but I feel I can suggest a few other clues, which may not have been thought of as important indicators to severe voices. These are completely based on my own experiences. I am not sure whether psychiatrists think of voices as being a standard fixed level experience; that is to say, one which is basically the same experience for one person whenever it happens, rather than a variable experience ranging from the mild to the severe.

The clues to 'bad' or severe voices are as follows:
1. Loudness of voices. Whether they are shouting, talking or whispering. Whether they are louder than people talking in the room.
2. Where the voices appear from. Are they in the head, the ears the room or broadcasting from afar? The longer the distance, the worse the voices.
3. Speed of words/lack of pauses. How fast are the voices talking? Are they too fast to be talked out? The faster the voices the worse they are.
4. Number of voices talking at once. Is it a single voice? Many voices is severe.

5. Thought insertion. When accompanied by the above symptoms this indicates severity and is a dangerous symptom which can lead to violence.
6. Disorder of volition. The extent to which I feel controlled and act out inserted thoughts. Also indicates the severity of my voices.
7. Bizarre restricted gait. A slow measured walk with stiff arms, legs and a hunched back (not to be confused with E.P.S.E.) is a sure sign of bad voices. Facial expression - furrowed brow.

These clues may all appear together, and the more that they appear the greater the severity of the experience. The bad voices may only be present for a short time, but this can be many times more distressing than a week of constant, mild, good voices. I believe that if these guidelines were used as indicators to the severity of my symptoms, a lot of understanding and suffering could be avoided.

AN1
13/1/94

17/3/98

A PERSONAL EXPERIENCE

The following charts Linda's mood swing which lasted six months, between September and March. She was high for three months. Following that she went into a depression, which also lasted three months, and then she came out of it.

The first piece was written a short while before Linda went into hospital.

> I'm feeling great! Life is so rich and I'm happy having
> so much energy and being so active and alive. My
> thoughts and feelings are intense, diverse and flow
> in a most satisfying way. It's pure pleasure to work.
> Anything I do is brilliant, thorough and efficient.
> I have trouble stopping! I feel very clear. I'm in
> control of something precious. I am so lucky to be
> experiencing this.

The second piece she wrote when she had 'come down' and slipped into depression throughout January, February and March.

> I feel awful. It's like being in pain. I dread doing anything
> and have great difficulty getting up and facing the day.
> I feel so miserable. Life isn't worth living like this.
> Mentally and physically I feel drained and I despair of ever
> feeling well again.

This is just one cycle of mood swings. This had been happening to Linda for eight years with one cycle after another. The gap in-between, when she feels well, varies from nothing up to a maximum of two months.

L. Cusick

ALEXANDER

I am 39 years of age and suffer from a mild form of schizophrenia. I imagine things and have irrational thoughts. I used to shout and scream and roar like a lion. I cried a lot.

Everybody laughs at me. I'm so funny. I'm a laugh a minute. I was in Severalls Hospital, Colchester from 1979 to 1984/1985. I used to live in Walton-on-the-Naze for 37 years until my father died in 1994. I was doing alright until this schizophrenia business started. I thought I was someone else. I would wet my blazer. I would hide other people's books. I would walk home from school (8 miles). I would not talk to my parents. I wanted to get 100 per cent in my 'O' levels. I kept on writing in rough.

In 1976 I left school. I had funny feelings of instability. I saw the consultant at Clacton Hospital in 1977. He accused me of attacking his consultant (he should have had me in hospital - instead he sent me to a half-way house in Colchester (Havengore)). I got a job at the fruit-farm, Fiveways, pushing trolleys at Stoneway. At the fruit farm I earned £1,000, which I put into shares. I did night sorting in Colchester for the post office for Christmas. So impressed were the management that they later offered me a job as a postman at Frinton-on-Sea. Then I worked at Boots in Colchester as a porter from 1978 to 1981. I walked around Colchester looking for work.

In 1979 I was too ill to work. I would run in front of cars. I would shout and scream and roar. In desperation I went to a doctor in Brinton-On-Sea. He gave me Haloperidol. I took the tablet. It made me ill. My tongue went blue. I was incontinent. My bed was wet with perspiration. I couldn't eat. My Dad had to hold me up in bed so that I could breathe. My parents called the doctor but he wouldn't come. In desperation my parents called an ambulance which took me to Essex County Hospital, Colchester. The nurse was horrified. The doctor said I was schizoid. They had to get an antidote from Severalls Hospital, Colchester. The result was that I put on weight. I was 20 stone. Everybody called me "slim". They shouted "you f*****g fat c***," out from their cars. Meanwhile, the doctor that gave me the tablet stopped me from socialising at Frinton Free Church. He also threatened to set his dog on me as I walked along the front at Frinton.

In 1982 I was 20 stone, had a painful infected wisdom tooth, and my parents were at their wits' end. I had left the shop I was working in in 1981 - because of my illness I was dismissed. I had cut the electric light ropes because they were strangulating me. I was in a terrible state. All green was dirty. The shop had to get rid of me.

I was desperate, I was in a crisis. I have always believed in providence, I turned on the T.V. What was on? A programme about schizophrenia, about a man on injections. I was inspired. I must have it. I went with the Social Worker to see the Consultant. I asked him, "Can I have an injection like I saw on T.V. please?" "No," was the answer. I stormed out of the room and started shouting, screaming and hollering. I went back to the room and said, "Can I have this injection?"

"No," he said again. I banged the table with my fists and roared at him. "Oh, very well," he said, and scribbled a prescription (he probably wanted to get rid of me.) He put me on Depixol, but my side swelled up, so they put me on Modelete. I had been on injections for 2 years. My C.P.N. was a woman. I was due an injection. She never turned up. I got into a state. My father took me into hospital to get an emergency injection. I phoned her up and she got nasty with me. I later found out that during the time she was supposed to give me my injection she was in bed with a man. In

1987 I was put on Sulpiride (the laughing tablet) and I have been on Sulpiride and Modelete Injections ever since. In 1996 I left Essex for Sussex. I have progressed since then. Snakes under pillows, axes behind doors, cyanide in the water supply, water everywhere - all gone.

Alexander Davidson

<u>MY DAILY DOSE</u>

I take my daily dose of medication
    A handful of pills, and my Cliff.
Together they always work a treat.
There's nothing that can beat
    My L, P, M and Cliff.
They help to uplift
    and see me through
When times are tough
    and I get to feel I've had enough.
The best medication of all is my Cliff.
    My spirits he can uplift -
        Even make me cry
            He's really nice, I sigh.
I feel I'm not alone
    As if I'm in part of his caring zone.

Margaret

TABLETS

Some people who have to take medication due to their mental health feel that it is a burden to keep having to take tablets. I must admit that it sometimes feels like all I do is pop pills. I know of people who have stopped taking their medication, but soon find that hospital beckons. Maybe taking tablets is a right old hassle, but I would rather take my medication and keep well than to threaten my well-being by the inconvenience of having to take tablets.

I believe that when I am ill it is all down to a chemical imbalance. Just as someone who doesn't drink milk would find their teeth may suffer due to a lack of calcium, I need to have lithium as I am lacking some chemical in my body.

I suffer from manic depression which means I have times when I can go very 'high', which is when I feel that I am full of confidence, get-up-and-go, there is nothing I can't achieve. I am just walking on air; life is a bowl of cherries.

Then there is the 'low' where I feel the complete opposite, life feels as if it is not worth living, everything is a burden, I am down in a black hole. What a mess! This is where the medicine called lithium comes into play. It is a drug which somehow knows what it means for a patient to feel 'normal', and is fantastic for me. On top of this drug, I also take prothiade, which is an antidepressant. You may well ask why I need an anti-depressant if lithium is meant to keep me stable. Well, lithium is not always 100% effective, and as in my case I also need an anti-depressant as I have tendencies to go 'low'. The doctor has to be careful when I am feeling low that he doesn't raise my prothiaden too much, as I have a tendency to go too high. The doctor has to find the right balance so I feel 'normal'.

Margaret

THE COPY TYPIST'S LAMENT

I wrote my poem. Nurtured it, brought it to life.
In one of my moments of creativity, the bonus of Manic Depression:
I typed it into the computer, savouring every nuance and change of mood.

Now I've lost my poem.
I've found the disc.
Recovered the second part - the ramblings of a whirling, busy, squiffy mind!
But where is the first part? I **know** it was good.

I can remember reading it to the lovely friend who supported me in my agony of insomnia.
It was appropriate, as her daughter is disabled and she knew what I meant.
Spewed into the bin.
Mountains of rubbish which I have accumulated in my insanity,
In the Civic Depot.

You may say I've found a new poem now.

But **I** know I've lost **my** poem.

It's gone.
That moment when all the joys and pleasures of creativity are wrapped in brown paper packaging and pill popping plastic...

Give up those pills?
Find my creativity again?
Or endure the milder peaks and troughs without the frisson of excitement?

Still, I can be useful, I dutifully take my 13 pills a day and act as copy typist with my computer...personally poem-less.
(After thought... What power these psychiatrists have).

CCT

TO RISPERIDONE

(An atypical anti-psychotic drug)

I am an atypical schizophrenic
and it is my belief
That modern neuroleptic drugs
Will bring us huge relief.

Millions of human beings
Who might feel they are in hell,
If put on the newer drugs
Might at last become well.

If the drug works as well for others
as it has done for me,
Then from pain and suffering
We might all be free.

Imagine the relief world-wide
as the pain and suffering passes
for about forty million people
of all colours, creeds and classes.

Imagine getting back your life
and having a future to come.
I now look forward to my future
in the next millennium!

Jim Wilson

MILD MANIA?

When I used to feel under stimulated
I used to go out and get inebriated.
I wanted a different kind of stimulation
Than was offered by a T.V. station.
I wanted to discuss the meaning of life
and along the way find myself a wife,
But all I got was inebriated
and I always ended up intoxicated.
Then would wake up next day in my own bed
with nothing more than a sore head.
Now I stay sober of a night
And think up rhyming poems to write.
By using my imagination as a source of self-stimulation
I get the inspiration to propel me to such a state of elation,
I feel close to the source of all creation!

(Then I take my prescribed medication
and go to bed to sleep under sedation
Then wake next day feeling healthier
to find myself another poem wealthier.)
(Even though it may not be great literature
For it I feel a whole lot richer.)

Jim Wilson

MIRROR IMAGES

Last Sunday I saw a programme by the BBC.
Which had a profound effect on me.
It brought an experience I had to mind
About when I had an audio and visual experience combined.
The programme, called 'Everyman', on T.V.
Brought back a time when an angel or alien visited me.
At first I thought the experience was just a hallucination
And just a figment of my imagination,
But, when I applied my intelligence
Then the experience began to make sense.
I had been in my bedroom in my bed
When the angel/alien appeared to me and said,
To benefit the human race
Put mirrors into space,
To flood Earth with light
So there's no more light'
I had the image of mirrors up in space
Orbiting our planet with celestial grace.
So I wrote to the Prime Minister of the time,
Though I didn't mention the angel/alien's rhyme,
The reply I got was very low key
And the Department of Energy didn't impress me.
So I wrote President Bush a letter
And the response I got was positively better.
Then some time later, much to my merriment,
Russians put a mirror in space as an experiment
From their 'Mia' space station,

Much to my delight and jubilation.
News of the experiment filled me with happiness
As the temporary mirror was a big success.
I still have telepathic hallucinations
And I pass these communications to radio stations,
Though I take an anti-psychotic drug called 'Risperidone',
I enjoy getting messages through my Cosmic Phone!

(I think 'Risperidone' is a wonderful form of medication
As it helps me to control my telepathic mode of communication.)

(Now I've drafted this rhyme
And the words are beginning to jingle
The hairs on the back of my neck
Are starting to tingle.
Once I've crafted this rhyme
And the images mingle
I wonder if it will still
Make my spine tingle.)

Jim Wilson

THANKS TO RISPERIDONE

I used to be in the butchery business,
But became a victim of my own success
as I was far from lazy,
But got so busy, I went crazy.
Our meat was so much in demand
We decided to expand,
Then through no fault of my own
I got a call down the cosmic phone
Which implanted altruistic concepts into my mind
Then sent me on a mission to save humankind.
The nature of my form of insanity
Awoke me to the suffering of humanity,
But, now I feel I'm in a position
to succeed in my messianic mission!

Jim Wilson

YELLOW STAR

Tomorrow there will be no ambulances
Tomorrow there will be no beds
Tomorrow Clopixol will be given by law

Today people are incapacitated by medicines
Today people are suffering the horrors of psychosis
Today people are refused care

Do we deserve life?
Why are we so intolerable?
Why don't we have the right to be safe?

The nurses are handing over
The doctors are mega dosing
They have great parties though

We are tormented in our cells, neglected and acuphased

Right now someone's having a Clopixol rebound
Right now someone's attempting suicide
Right now we are treated like Jews in the war by Nazis, it's just
more subtle

Remove our homes, our hospital, put us on psychoactive sub-
stances
Give us no support, ignore us
We are dying, we have no place
How many suicides can they ignore?

And what are the issues that have been created?

That we are the dangerous schizophrenics
That the community needs protecting from

We have no lives we exist
The Community cannot accept us, it destroys us
It's what we need protections from

Who suffers? The woman whose son has been killed by a schizophrenic? The woman who still works, cooks, has pleasure, reads copes and often cries to release her natural grief?

Or the thousands upon thousands of vulnerable, tortured, people
Whose suffering is untold, who are stigmatised, medicated, neglected, Psychotic, depressed?

Who have no friends, no place in this society, no hospitals,
Who are invisible, having been absorbed into the world that
Destroys them, who live lives of suffering unimaginable.

We have no voice, but our collective would say, **ASYLUM**
The badge of the decided **unliveable, intolerable**
Was the yellow star, the shaven head, the pink triangle

What is it now?
     Who do we wish to **cleanse?**
The badge of the decided **unliveable, intolerable**
Is the Clopixol neck
The Lergactyl shuffle
The dead eyes of Stelazine

The Lithium paunch
The restless legs of Modecate
The Parkinsons disease of Haloperidol
The vegetation
The destruction of intelligence by antipsychotics

Is it better for us to be mentally retarded,
And physically debilitated than to be insane?

Please let us be what we are (I hear no one listening)

AN2
30/10/96

7. THE DOVE CENTRE (Chelmsford and District MIND):

7a Creative Writing Group

THE DOVE CENTRE
CREATIVE WRITING GROUP

These poems have been written by people who attend the Dove Centre, now known as MIND. They all suffer from depression.

The following poems were written on the theme of:

The Secret Crier.
He didn't want to cry in secret
He wanted the whole wide world to know
How desolate he felt inside
His feelings with nowhere to hide.
Come and share my hurt within me
or take it and shut it away, no more to see
Hold my body and heal my pain
Do not leave me crying in vain.
No one is there though No one cares
Cry and cry and drop out the tears
Drop out the tears and release the fears.

JANET

Alone I weep solitary tears
The pain of rejection so raw
So near and deep and crippling
but I've felt this pain before
Like a baby left helpless
Unwanted, unfed, unloved
Once before I was that baby
My mother wanted no more.

HELEN

The tiny bent old lady
Drew the translucent nets to feel the knives drawn
The sharpest one her son.
Such pain she hides in fear
The paining is worth a fortune
The family want her in a home
Just because she is 'strange'
And the painting can hang in another place.
Condemned for being different
Her greatest treasure already lost
and she the sacrificial lamb.

JANIS

She wept inside
Needing the comfort of the world
Except it was a secret
He didn't know.
She couldn't face him that day
Lying in his hospital bed.
Now it was over
She was relieved he had found out
Facing his final days together
Rather than alone.

MARY

Oh yes I'm fine
She said and smiled
A false bright smile
That might have fooled.
Discerning eyes
Might see a brightness

Telling of tears unshed.
Most took her at face value
Never seeing
The lake of tears inside
Product of years of fear, of guilt of life unfulfilled.

ELSPETH

Alone that night
She cried and no one heard
She didn't mind
When he was there
She cried in secret
So quiet he never heard
And never knew.
It's not correct to cry aloud
She felt that it was easier to keep it to herself.

SYLVIA

The boy was caught. He'd been doing wrong
to the headmaster's office
He was duly marched
The punishment decreed
It had to be met.
Swish went the cane
His flesh felt the pain
He wanted to shout
He wanted to cry
This was a no no.
What would his mates think -
A wimp through and through.

DEREK

My sorrow broke
My eyes were sore with weeping torrents as never before
The pain of grief
Nauseous and sad
Oh why oh why
Is life so bad?
Why did he have to leave me so
and break my tender heart
I didn't ask for all this pain
Please, never come near me again.

PAM C.

Her little arms
Hid her face
Corner sheltered
She sat and cried.
Secret idyll,
Her own room.
Cruel remarks and vicious shoving.
The tears had fallen before
and now she knew to hide her grief.
Alone, she felt alone.

EMMA

8. PROFESSIONALS HAVE THEIR SAY

A TYPICAL DAY

I arrive at the Linden Centre at nine a.m. The fact that I have to take my children to school in the mornings makes it easier to be punctual. I would most probably be late otherwise, as I hate waking up early.

Before delving into the day-to-day work, I usually make my secretary a cup of coffee.

Only once in ten months did she do it for me, and I shall never forget that day.

When the first patient arrives for the clinic appointment, I watch his or her face with big curiosity, to see even before they tell me how they feel, if I can guess their frame of mind. It is lovely when I see a beaming face, but a tearful one makes me feel that our profession is worthwhile.

Patient after patient disclose to me their innermost secrets and, believe me, I get to hear the most incredible stories.

Sometimes I need to go to the ward and it is then when I meet the people who for a shorter or longer time-span need to be in hospital to recharge their batteries.

What I find amongst the most unpleasant situations in psychiatry, is the fact that some of the patients on sections of the Mental Health Act regard us psychiatrists as their enemies, although deep down I know that it is in their best interest to be kept in hospital against their will. I hope that better and better treatments will be discovered soon to help patients get better quicker and enjoy the life outside the hospital.

Anonymous Psychiatrist

CARING FOR THE MIND

There is still a great lack of understanding of mental illness in our society and an even greater lack of proper provision for the care of the mentally ill.

The tragic death of Christopher Edwards, beaten to death by a schizophrenic cellmate in Chelmsford Prison, has highlighted these problems. Christopher's killer was a severely mentally ill person. An inquiry reports blamed multiple failures by the authorities. Action must be taken, but nothing will bring back Christopher or erase the shock of his death from his grieving parents.

There is a fear of mental illness which makes people less sympathetic than they would be to someone with an obvious physical illness or disability. Sometimes there is just plain hostility. This makes those who do suffer from mental ill health and their families even more isolated and burdened.

Yet nearly four out of ten people ask for help with a mental health problem at some time in their lives. Doctors and counsellors find more and more people coming to them with emotional and mental problems which cause them as much distress as physical problems, sometimes more.

Though some forms of advanced mental illness clearly need expert help, many of the problems of stress, depression, anxiety and panic are needlessly aggravated by society's harsh and uncaring attitudes. These problems could be alleviated by greater kindness, patience, gentleness and good manners. People with mental health problems are often made to feel guilty and even shameful in a way no cancer patient would be.

John's gospel tells us that Jesus "knew what was in a man". His understanding of human frailty in all its aspects was complete, and he had no fear. He experienced the tortured mind (Gethsemane) and he was profoundly moved by all suffering. This compassion drove him to heal as well as to proclaim God's love.

We do need more resources for better care in the community for the mentally ill, but we also need the Christ-like attitude of compassion for all who suffer in this way.

This in itself would bring healing to hurt lives. Perhaps that will come when we are more honest with ourselves and one another about our mental health.

Rev. Keith Holloway

DES

Project Manager, Rainbow Clubhouse.

To say something about my role, I feel I must identify how I got to where I am in the mental health field at present. Here is a brief summary of my working experience in mental health: I began my career at the age of twenty-nine, with my first job being a nursing assistant on nights at Runwell Hospital. I felt I needed to try this work before undertaking student nurse training, just from the perspective of getting my feet wet before diving in. So in May 1987 I began my training with ten other student nurses in my class, with an initial induction block of seven weeks. This was spent entirely in the school of nursing, which was supposed to prepare us for our first allocation on an acute admission ward, ha ha! However, three years later I managed to not only survive, but to pass my state finals and become a registered mental nurse.

My first job as a Staff Nurse was on a rehabilitation ward providing care for thirty clients. I stayed there for six months and then moved on to a community based unit. Richmond Lodge was a twelve-bedded registered nursing home, implementing a philosophy of rehabilitation. After five years and a couple of promotions, I left to open a registered residential home in North Chingford, providing accommodation for people moving out of Claybury Hospital. Then in February 1996, I started work at Rainbow Clubhouse as Deputy Manager, and, in November 1997, I became Project Manager.

My role now as a Project Manager at Rainbow Clubhouse is to enable and empower members to take an active role in running their own Clubhouse Service. This involves me being approachable, with a good/bad sense of humour. I also have to co-ordinate and supervise the rest of the staff, ensuring that Clubhouse standards and principles are followed.

24 February 1998
Rainbow Clubhouse has since closed.

9. DEDICATION:

9a A religious word

CLIFF AND ME

Cliff Richard has helped me a lot. When I first heard the album 'Now You See Me, Now You Don't' it was like magic. I would listen to it over and over again. The words and music were fantastic. I really felt for the first time that here was someone who could produce an album that was religious but not dull, and that didn't contain insincere lyrics.

Over the years I have followed Cliff and have heard him talk about his faith. I just feel you can't fault the man. I'm sure like all of us he would say he's not perfect, but then who is? It is so interesting to listen to his interpretation of what being a Christian is all about. My faith is very important to me and when I am ill I need to hear and see Cliff as the Christian he is. Many people may look at him and see a good-looking, very pleasant man, but to me he is much more. He lives his life as true to his beliefs as he can. He lives along the lines of a true Christian and that's what attracts me.

When I am ill I need to have someone who I can look up to and lean on. Through his faith, he fills me with all the security I need when I don't understand what is happening in my world. Everything gets tossed upside down, but I have Cliff and he is my most special friend, even though he doesn't know me.

Margaret

CLIFF MANIA

I remember back to when I was in hospital in the early 80's. I met a girl called Jane and we got on really well. She let me listen to her Cliff Richard cassette called 'Now You See Me, Now You Don't', which I later found out is a Christian album. I found I could not hear enough of it - my Cliff Richard mania was born! It was just fantastic. I have always had a faith, and hearing Cliff sing was just magic. It was great music and great words which meant so much to me. It was as if I was in the depths of despair with my illness, and Cliff had brought God to me - or vice versa. Over the coming years, I found that I had caught a bug! I felt I needed to hear a lot more of his work. I listened to his music, and I couldn't wait to get to hear him talk about the way he felt about things.

Margaret

GOD SPOT

My faith is very important to me, so I'd like to take this opportunity to share my thoughts from the past and present with you.

1993-4 (Typed 21.7.96)

What is it all for? I ask myself, surely God has led me down this path for some reason? Or has He? What happens to us? Perhaps it's not of God's doing. I believe God gives us life and He gives us a free life to live and things that happen are because of that freedom. Adam (Adam and Eve) ate the apple so we have a life to choose how we live. I feel in life that through what we experience we can pray to God to ask Him to make good of the experiences we encounter. With the things I have experienced, surely God can help me turn them into something good.

Depression, why? Maybe there's things we do that we are unaware of which cause it. When Jesus was on earth, He did things that today we can understand and have a scientific reason for. Why shouldn't it be possible?

God knows everything, and all the things Jesus did are probably possible for us to do, with learning. Where does space end? One day we may find the answer. The point I am making is just because man understands how things that Jesus did are done doesn't disapprove his validity. Everything that God can do has a logical reason behind it. Why shouldn't it be possible for us to understand how things God does are done? He made man, then gave us intelligence. Things we can do now, like turning on a light, would be a miracle if we travelled back to Jesus' time. Why should our understanding of these things make Jesus less that what we believe He was - the Son of God?

Many years ago, a friend said her family didn't believe in God because a relation was in an airplane in the war and was shot down and killed. She blamed God - but who invented aeroplanes and bombs? Man chose to invent these things. God gives us knowledge to use for good or for bad - if man chooses to build things that kill, then whose fault is it? God gives man the freedom to choose, why doesn't man make inventions to spread peace instead of war?

Margaret

HOW CAN THERE BE A GOD?

How can I suffer as much as I do and still be able to believe in God? Some people may ask. Surely there can't be a loving God up there if He allows me to continue to have this mental illness with all the desperation and pain I go through?

So why do I still believe in Him? Well I feel that in this life most of us suffer in one way or another. It says in the bible that 'Adam disobeyed God by eating the forbidden fruit - he had the choice of obeying God, but he chose to do what he wanted to do. So I believe today life cannot be perfect because of Adam's choice. God gives us freedom to live as we wish to. Many illnesses, even today, we find we have to suffer, but if you believe in God, He can be there if you ask Him to, and He will help. I believe it is in the way you tackle problems. I find with God's help, He can make all the difference.

As an example, I was feeling low again and I was just so cross with God. I felt that He was letting me down in a big way. So I made an emergency appointment with the doctor. When I saw him I was just amazed that he had the result of a blood test that I had had only the previous day for my lithium tablets! He was then able to increase the dose I was taking, and I just felt so good, as my doctor is always so kind and caring. Maybe this new dose of tablets may take up to two weeks to be fully effective, but I just felt so much better for just seeing my doctor that day. So now I can thank God for His help with this situation. I find God always comes up trumps somehow, if you let Him.

Margaret

<u>JESUS</u>

There came a time when I was afraid nothing would work - nothing to see me through the dark, lonely days of depression. It was suggested that at these time I should turn to Jesus and ask Him to have mercy on me. So I tried it, and it worked! In the past there had often been a void that no one could fill, but turning to Jesus, I felt an overabundance of love and hope. Jesus is forever, He is love, there is no void there, only love that is always there - FOREVER.

Margaret

NOW YOU SEE ME. NOW YOU DON'T

Since the time I had an introduction to Cliff Richard's spiritual side through the album 'Now You See Me, Now You Don't', I have never felt alone. When no one understood me due to my illness, I knew I wouldn't feel alone as I had Cliff to stand by me through his love of God. When it felt like I was in my darkest hour of despair and rejection, through the album 'Now You See Me, Now You Don't', Cliff's love for God came across clearly. It is God that I feel close to through Cliff. The words and music are very uplifting and mean a great deal to me. I find I can sing, and even dance to the tracks on the album. The words are very sincere and they praise God. I can join in and feel at one with Cliff as a link to God.

Margaret

SOUL MATES

Many years ago, when I was first ill, my family found my illness hard to cope with. As it was mental illness and not physical, and so cannot be seen, the illness was just existing inside of me. It was hard to understand what was wrong with me. As they became more concerned and exasperated by my behaviour, all they could see was that I was behaving neurotically. Why was she behaving in such a way?

In the early days I didn't know who to turn to and I ended up very lonely with everyone including myself, exhausted and at our wits' end as to knowing how to cope with all this. I felt that their behaviour towards me was aggressive. Hospital usually followed.

One time when I was in hospital I met a girl called Jane, she had an album of Cliff Richard's called 'Now You See Me Now You Don't'. It was magic - it was music to my ears! It was great. I was to learn more and more about the wonders of Cliff.

It was so good - I had found a soul-mate. I could see him on video, hear him on my stereo, conveying messages through his lyrics that God's love was there for everyone. He came across as a gentle, caring, loving human being whose core was an interpretation of God's love. Cliff follows God's Word and conveys Christianity to the full. He allows the Word of God to shape his very being.

So when the going gets tough and there is madness going on, and it feels as though I am so alone, I can turn to Cliff. I seem to feel he comforts me and he cares about me. He sings about 'you and me'. He makes me feel as though I am the 'you'. As time goes I get to feel more and more close to Cliff, to feel he really does care - which is because of my illness. I find it difficult hearing Devil Woman and I guess it brings me back to appreciate my family. I realise how much I need and love my husband and daughter.

I become embarrassed about my obsession with Cliff - and totally fed up of hearing Cliff sing! I'm glad for a break from Cliff. Later on I go back to seeing him for exactly what he is for me: an extra-ordinarily wonderful warm person who carries on caring, singing meaningful songs - and acting the clown! He is always so careful with what he says and he conveys God's love through everything he does.

At the end of the day I believe he is a wonderful example of what being a Christian is all about. I believe I am able to feel God's love through him.

Margaret

WHY AS A CHRISTIAN SHOULD I SUFFER FROM MANIC DEPRESSION?

I believe God gives us life and He gives us a free hand to live life as we wish, and therefore things happen because of that freedom. It is said that in the beginning Adam ate the apple against God's wishes, Adam made that choice. Today we have a choice of how we want to live. Maybe because of the way we choose to live today, we may not be helping to improve our mental health.

Depression. Why? When Jesus was on this earth, He did things that today we can understand and have a scientific reason for. Why shouldn't it be possible? God knows everything, and all the things Jesus did are probably possible for us to learn to do. I sometimes wonder where does space end? One day we may find the answer. The point I am making is just because man understands today how things Jesus did are done doesn't disprove the validity of them. Everything that God can do there is a logical reason for. Why shouldn't it be possible for us to understand how things God does are done? He made man, then gave him intelligence. Things we can do now, like turn on a light, would be a miracle if we travelled back to Jesus's time. As far as depression is concerned, I'm sure one day we will fully understand why people have to suffer from it. Mental illness has been around a very long time and the matter has often been swept under the carpet. Unless more people show more interest in it, then maybe we may never fully understand it. I hope through this book that eyes may be opened. I feel that many people suffer from mental illness, many of whom keep it to themselves, and therefore the enormity of this problem is underestimated.

Margaret

9. DEDICATION:

9b Faith

IN GOD WE MUST TRUST

There are so many questions
　　Without enough answers,
Who am I to say why?
How can things happen to us who believe?
　　Without there being an answer from God?
He holds the cards
　　And He plays; in ways we may not understand.
When all seems wrong and we feel it's so right.

When Noah built his ark
　　No one believed him.

We have to trust God,
　　Who are we to question Him?
I am lost in a battle.
　　I feel confused.
Surely God must know,
　　It's in His plan.
I trust Him and pray.

When God and the Devil
　　Fight for the right of my conscious.
　　I pray God will win.
If we trust in Him
　　He can't lose.
Cause He's the one
　　Whose power is divine.

We just must trust as He is the way,
The truth,
And the light.

Margaret

DARKNESS AND LIGHT

Take my mind that stands alone
Take my heart before I roam
Oh God you taught me love
and you taught me pain
You also had me back again
God give me a chance to come to you.

In all the darkness and light,
you are my strength for my soul
What an honour to be told

Bob Lewis

HELP ME LORD

Help me Lord, on this troubled day
　　To remember to turn to you and pray.
"Please help," is all I need to ask
　　Somehow He will put all my troubles in the past.
He will lift those grey clouds, so blue skies follow
　　and find, in time I no longer have to wallow
　　　　in a state of troubled mind.
With God I know I will soon find
　　He's always been there to show me the way
　　　　When all I needed to do was pray.

Margaret

IN REMEMBRANCE OF CONNIE

Once I was diagnosed as crazy
Because the world's pain was mine
My touch with reality became hazy
and I believed my will divine.

In hospital I saw around me
Faces full of fear, of mistrust
in private places of the psyche
Private hells where demons thrust.

I experienced hellish foes
Powers too strong to conquer alone;
And the added fears of others' woes
Stripped me naked to the bone.

The doctors and nurses stood apart
Telepathy was just for the mad
We shared a violation of the heart
We could not say this made us glad.

I tried to escape - I was shut in
A room of mattress and four walls;
I marched to fight the bitter sin
The time of reckoning when judgement calls.

My judges of heaven and hell
Each claiming dominion of my soul

Each step I took the further
I fell till I lost sight of heaven's goal.

I became calm in realisation
That I wasn't divine at all
But a product of creation
One of God's children, but not of St. Paul.

Then I proved my mortality
by pissing on the shining ground;
I had no thought of immorality
but only a desperate need was found.

Soon after they opened the door
and a black shining face I saw
Shining with compassion and love;
I was the fiend and she the dove.

She did not seem to notice my sin
or the broken fabric of my heart;
But fed me two dinners and kept vigil
as if my needs were hers, in part.

God sent me an angel after the storm
and I knew I had survived;
Though diminished I was reborn
with an angel by my side.

I loved her then and still
for she did not judge me mad
She did not judge me at all
Just a friend to one in need.

Now I appear to be well and alone
for I do not flinch at other's pain;
And their fears are not my own
But I'm bereft, for my child was slain.

Christine S

JESUS

But still I kept in hiding
    Unsure and very afraid
        But Jesus showed
            Me life and I came
                Out of the cave.

Jesus has the victory and is
    Very much alive.
        But Satan wouldn't
            Let me be until
                I cried in <u>Christ's</u> name.

                        Jane Newman

MANIC DEPRESSION TAKES ITS GRIP

Are you really a friend or foe?
　　There comes a time when I feel I don't really know.
Your annoyance at all the things I am doing,
　　Using the computer and video I am viewing.
Watching Cliff and hearing him sing -
　　I know you'd love to just throw them all in the bin!
At times like this I feel very much alone -
　　This illness inside me has very much grown.
I end up in hospital where I need to rest -
　　We've all decided it's really for the best.
Reality eventually dawns.
My husband and daughter I can now see,
　　The love is real that they feel for me.
Thank you God, I must pray,
　　I never thought I would reach this day.

Margaret

MICHELLE AND I

I was blessed with a baby girl.
She was all that I could have ever wanted.
I loved her dearly.
But soon I was to find
    Mental Illness would grasp my very being and leave me feeble and weak.
        Just a pathetic shell, was all that there was left.
It seemed as if all I was left with was confusion
    And for me to somehow play my part in her world.
How did I survive with all the responsibility on my shoulders?
    I do not know.
I only thank God today
    That together, my daughter and I
      Are here to tell the tale.
I love my beloved daughter, Michelle
    and I marvel at what God has done
      In helping me to see this day.
With her along beside me, He has kept us safe
    And united through those turbulent years.

                        Margaret

GOD, THREE IN ONE

Words and music by Carol Smith   **©Carol Smith 1997**

GOD, THREE IN ONE

God the Father, God the Son, the Holy Spirit the three in one

Written by a former member of the Dove Centre (now known as MIND)

Chelmsford.

The Dove Centre is no longer in Chelmsford.

THANK GOD!

God viewed the planet and He said that it was good.
But Adam let Him down with the bite of an apple.
Adam started the role of events
    That led to God's dismay.
One man was to come and show us the way.
Sent from God, Jesus came.
    But the rot was set, and the cross beckoned.
Now Jesus is welcomed home.
    He is reunited with His Father.
Jesus came to show us the way
    And we can follow, so that one day
        We will all be able to see
            The glory of eternal life and a perfect existence.

Margaret

QUESTIONS

There are so many questions
    Without enough answers.
Who am I to say why?
How can things happen to us who believe,
       Without there being an answer from God.
He holds the cards
    And He plays, in ways we many not understand.
When all seems wrong
    And we feel it's so right.
When Noah built his ark:
    No-one believed him.
We have to trust God.
    Who are we to question Him?

I am lost in a battle
I feel confused
Surely God must know:
    It's in his plan.
I trust Him
    And pray.
When God and the Devil
    Fight for the right of my conscious
       pray God will win.
If we trust in Him
    He can't lose,
Cause He's the one
Whose power is Divine
We just must trust as He is the way, the truth and the light.

               Margaret

WHY

This man has lost a limb,
This other has but half a mind,
And still a bird with a broken wing
Sings sweetly to the sky.

God in heaven, answer me.
Why this dreadful cruelty
That tears the heart
And blinds the eye?

IF heaven were the shape of suffering,
I'd enter in if love were there.
For paradise without my love
Is but a golden desert bare.

I made you learn to love my loss,
I bared my soul upon the cross.
For love to share
I suffered there.

Christine S

10. AT PEACE:

10a Friends

MILLION

There is proof
That you
Are one in a million.

I thought I was special
Cynically
How poetic
that I met you.

Now I don't mean to patronise
but both our stories sound tragic
Still believing in fairy-tales.

How sad we laughed
but how rich
It has been
for that meeting.
You told me.

Things I have been known to tell
I held you
The way I wanted to be held.

I won't tell you my story
and I love you.

Audra Gardner

HOPEFULLY

A bleak cold day
made from the warmth
left behind of yesterday's sun
will be tomorrow's beginning.

Children made from
man's endeavours
watch today with hollow eyes.

Trees are going,
so are flowers, newts
and telegraph poles.
What we have left
is what we make
but friends hold no time
and years are only what
you want them to be.

Fuzz
26.4.96

A FRIEND IN NEED

Disbelief, anguish, pain, helplessness, frustration - just some of the feelings that, as a good friend and Godmother to her only child, hit me the first time Margaret's depression got the better of her.

Over the eighteen years since Margaret's depression was first diagnosed, I, as a good friend, have suffered with her. Not as much as Stewart and Michelle, but nevertheless the feelings described in the first line grip me every time her depression grips her.

Having had depression in the past myself, I can honestly say I don't think the sufferer ever realises just how much of an effect the condition has on those close to them, usually those we love and would not normally hurt. People around who don't suffer would say the one in depression 'has nothing to be depressed about' but that usually means nothing materially to be depressed about. What sets depression off initially (speaking personally) is a feeling of worthlessness, lack of self-esteem and lack of self-confidence, and thinking that you don't make any difference to life - but that just isn't true.

Once out of the 'black hole' of depression, and with the love of those around you, we should be able to see that each and every one of us has something to give in life. In the eyes of God, we all are equal, and that is how it should be. No-one has the right to make another feel worthless, stupid or useless, but it is not usually the people that make you feel like that that suffer, but the one it is aimed at, usually the 'weaker'.

We can't all make the BIG difference in the world, but we can all make SOME difference whilst on this earth, and that is what we all need to make depressed people believe and feel - that they are just as valuable and special as anyone else, and loved just as much.

Ann G. Levett **18.2.98**

IT'S GOOD TO TALK

When life gets really tough and you feel you've had enough
It's too easy to cure your ills by swallowing a bottle of pills
It is then you must be strong as better days will come along
It doesn't mean that you are weak if you feel the need to speak.
I have found it's always best to get my troubles off my chest.
Just find a friend who will lend an ear
Or speak to someone who is willing to hear
As more honest, two-way communication
Is the key to humankind's salvation!

Jim Wilson

KATY

My first experience of mental illness was when I attended St. John Payne Secondary School. I had a best friend called Katy. I remember she was full of life and we had a very happy friendship. We got on really well. Then I remember we were in a science class one morning and she seemed to go into a shell. Katy was just doodling. Soon after she had a stay in Severals Hospital, and her mum took me to visit her. Our friendship changed. She became quite snappy, and I soon learnt to be careful with what I said to her. I really felt I had been cheated out of my old pal, but we were friends, and friends stick together. I think over the years Katy has done really well. I feel that life really improved for her when she had her son, Christopher. She seemed to bloom. I was really pleased for her. Now she is married to Chris and has a daughter, Rosanna. I feel life is now complete for her, especially now she has found faith in God. Life must be perfect. It's all really wonderful for her.

Margaret

VOICE ON THE RADIO

Thank you dear voice on the radio.
I listen and I can relax.
Your tone soothes
    this never ending state of turmoil.

Thank you dear voice on the radio.
You let me know I'm not alone
    for silence to me, or the company
        of insensitive people is more than I could bear.

I have a dear friend
    who helps to smooth the most wretched of hours.
She cares and says just what I need to hear
    but I cannot talk to her all the time,
        so at least I have my voice on the radio.

Margaret

MY FRIEND DOROTHY

I would like to say that one of the 'nice' things about this illness is friends. I first met my friend Dorothy in 1980 when I was expecting my daughter, Michelle. She was the wife of Keith, the new vicar in the village. Over the years we've built up a wonderful friendship. They say that when you're in need, you certainly know who your friends are, and Dorothy is one of mine. I'd like to pay tribute to her. Dorothy has helped me a great deal. At one time when I was ill I used to go round to see her every Monday morning. We would sit together talking and usually prepared things for Sunday school. I remember when I was frustrated with the way I was feeling she gave me a cushion to punch, which only helped a little, but it was good of her to try and help. One time I was in a terrible state so I phoned up another friend who asked if I wanted her to phone Dorothy. She did, and Dorothy wasted no time in rushing round to see me in my hour of need. More recently I found myself in an awful way first thing in the morning, and on one occasion I phoned Dorothy up in desperation. She was wonderful. Since then, I know at any time I can phone her, and it is truly wonderful. She seems to say all the things I need to hear. Many times she has helped me to carry on.

Dorothy has always had time for me and acts very much as a good Christian should.

These days Dorothy and her husband, Keith now live away from the Village. She still doesn't give up caring for me. When I am ill, she is quite happy for me to phone her up at 7.45 a.m. when my daughter has left for college and I am feeling at my worst. I speak to her for a short while when I'm in total desperation and even though she hasn't suffered from depression, she always knows the right things to say to me. She really is a tower of strength to me when I am finding life is impossible to live with. She assures me it won't last forever and tells me that I am doing well despite the way I feel. After speaking to her for a short while each weekday morning, it is just enough to get me though that very difficult time and gives me strength and determination to carry on with my day. I don't know where I would be without her.

There are other friends who have helped me along the way. One friend of mine, who I mentioned earlier, is Jane. We don't see each other very often, but she has helped when I really needed it. When I've been in hospital I have received many cards and some letters, and some visits from people. I kind of feel that if I wasn't ill, I would not feel the level of care some people feel for me. Just recently when I was feeling bad and crying all the time, people at the Rainbow Clubhouse where I go were showing me such care and affection. Some put their arms around me, some speak warmly and encouragingly. Mental illness is not what anybody wants, but through it so much is given to us.

Margaret

The Rainbow Clubhouse has since closed

10 AT PEACE:

10b Moving in the right direction

TITANIC

Some time ago I noticed there was an outing with the Rainbow Clubhouse that I attend to go to see the film 'Titanic'. At first I wasn't at all interested in going as I was feeling low (I suffer from manic depression). I find when I am feeling low everything seems very difficult to cope with. I find I need to stick to my routine, and especially in the evening I feel I need to be at home watching the T.V., and that's how I felt at first. A week before the evening out, I found I was feeling quite a lot better, and the thought of an evening at the pictures at that time seemed very tempting. I felt very brave adding my name to the list of people who were going to attend this venture. When I reached the day I was feeling alright and in the end I had a really good evening out. We all went in cars to the cinema in Thurrock, and I found I thoroughly enjoyed the evening out. It just felt so good to be able to feel so relaxed and to enjoy the evening as much as I did. The film went on for about three hours, but all the time I felt glued to the screen and I just became engulfed in it. It was a love story with the elderly lady recalling the events she experienced as she was a survivor of the tragedy. When I am feeling well, life is just so wonderful, and it really makes you appreciate how wonderful life can be.

Margaret

The Rainbow Clubhouse is no longer in Chelmsford.

WHY WE SUFFER

I make no secret
That I've been mentally ill
and for the past seventeen years
I've been climbing up a hill

Now even though
Twice a day I take a pill
I think I have reached
The top of my hill

I now see before me
A vast level plane
with many sign posts
to keep me sane.

You can come too
If you feel inclined
as there is an open door
for all humankind

When you get there
You will find Happiness
and peace of mind

Pain and suffering
Will be no more
When you walk

Through the door.

There will be light
And you will understand
Why suffering exists
When you reach the promised land.

For if you knew no pain
Suffering and grief,
How would you know
The joy of relief?

So it is my
Fundamental Belief
We should not cause suffering
but, try to bring relief.

And if we were all to work
With this aim in mind
Earth would be a better place
For humankind!

Jim Wilson

WRITTEN IN A 'DROP-IN'

My bizarre beliefs keep me going
Like being in a river that keeps on flowing.
Sometimes I flow swiftly and shallow
And my thoughts are like a field in fallow,
Then I run with thoughts that are deep
And, sometimes, personal insights I reap.
Then as I flow I've often found
Myself go over well worn ground
And as over time most things change
I often discover my beliefs are not so strange.
Having been a 'dropout' from college,
I am a man of limited knowledge,
But, as each day I keep on flowing
I find myself to continue growing
and, perhaps, if I keep myself in motion
Someday, I may become more than just
A drop in the ocean!

Jim Wilson

ACROSS THE WILDERNESS

Recently I saw a man on T.V.
Whose words had a profound effect on me.
He described having an auditory hallucination which sent him
on the road to his salvation.
He had been in the depths of despair
When a 'voice' told him we all have a cross to bear.
Then his burden of depression began to ease,
Now he is helping children overseas.
Some may find their cross too heavy a load and fall by the way-
side of the road,
I say to you do not despair as I've been there,
Now I feel like I walk on air
And I am willing to lend a hand
To help us all get to the promised land!

Jim Wilson

10 AT PEACE:

10c Things are going well

DO OR DIE

Do or die,
But always ours to reason why,
why there is no reason to die
Without reason to live,
born to live and give life,
So we must live this life,
to the full,
And not just Do or Die.

Simon G

THE OTHER SIDE OF PSYCHOSIS

At twenty-four years old
I went into 'psychosis'
And they gave me 'schizophrenia'
As the diagnosis.

Ever since then
as far as I've been able
I've worked hard
To demise that catastrophic label.

Ever since then
I've tried to be sensible
And tried to understand 'schizophrenia'
So as it became comprehensible.

'Psychosis' may be described as a mental derangement,
But, after it, if you rebuild your values into a new arrangement.

There are insights into the universe
as being one giant organism
and concepts so complicated
I'd need to use more than a neologism.

To describe the wonders,
Which are beyond just imagination,
Of this universe
And its driving force of creation!

Jim Wilson

A WORD SALAD?

Though I feel well, perhaps,
I'm heading for a cataclysmic relapse.
Perhaps the world I've built over the years
Will collapse about my ears.
Perhaps the universe is a hallucination
and just a figment of my imagination.
Concepts come into my human brain
for which there are no words to explain.
I find myself a runner in the human race
When my reality lies in time and space.
You may think I'm as mad as a hatter
as I run through this world of matter,
But, as I live with humanity
One day, I know, I will find lasting sanity!

Jim Wilson

HEARING VOICES

A Hearer's Perspective

25.03.1998

There are many explanations
For the phenomenon called auditory hallucinations
Telepathy, aliens, spirits, the voice of the soul,
The key is to learn to exercise control.
Try to make the lower order of voices go away
and keep the jokers and tricksters at bay.
Negative sides, we should learn to ignore
and bring positive aspects to the fore.
The secret is not to lose sight of free will
Otherwise the listener might become 'mentally ill'.
Read up about the 'Bicameral Mind'
And further the progress of humankind.
Hearing voices is not always a sign of insanity,
It is more, a different perception of reality.
I think it is a fascinating facet of the human brain
and don't write off hearers as being insane.
Instead, I think, everyone will gain good spirit guides
Which will help people to grow by their sides,
Once the powers of good achieve domination
Over those who would seek damnation
and, I think, this momentous day will come
Someday soon in the new millennium!

Jim Wilson

MAKER AND BAKER

I feel I've had someone by my side
Who has acted as a mentor and guide.
I'm not saying it has been an easy ride,
For a long time, I've been swimming against the tide,
But, I've often felt that the destiny of my soul
Has been out with my conscious control.
I feel under the influence of a cosmic force
Which comes from some kind of divine source.
Of course, this lack of volition or total free will
Has resulted in me being labelled 'mentally ill',
But, if my life had been shaped any other way
I wouldn't be the person that I am today
And with the feeling of 'at oneness', I feel tonight,
I feel like a cake that's about to turn out just right!

Jim Wilson

LIFE AND WORRY

Life and worry
are inseparable
The end of one is
The end of the other

But it is not of the human
to discount the worry
however self-destructive

An emotion as
this brought from
conscience guilt or fear
is something with which we live
Brought forth from many places

We do but try to grow
above it alone but better
with the care of others

And thus to attain the
Utopia of inner peace

Fuzz 15/1/97

THE MOOD RIDDLE

In His infinite wisdom it seems
It was one of God's great schemes
to invent emotional extremes
in our conscious thought and dreams

So we have times when are low,
Feeling negative and full of woe
There are days when we feel depressed
and sometimes so down we are distressed

Or we can feel positive and bright,
Our spirits are relaxed and light.
Or even feel so happy and high
We are ready to touch the sky.

Then I think in this great scheme
Most people are neither extreme,
In opinion it would seem
Most people are in between.

They do not feel too much sadness
nor are they overflowing with gladness
to get to the point of this riddle,
Most people are somewhere in the middle.

So I would like to do a shift
And see most people get a lift

Towards the happy end of the mood spectrum
And think this will come in the new millennium!

Jim Wilson

SMILE

Smile that is open wide
funny faces different places
long and wide
some up some down
but all meaning the same
Smile, things are not so bad
Look now and you will see
The real you
See how it makes you laugh
Wasn't so bad
Now was it? ha ha,
Laughter all the way now
Even if a little strange
but it works,
Go on have a go
Smile.

Laura Sorrell

I HAVE LOVE

Oh what joy I feel today
    I feel so very well.
My husband and daughter
    Are by my side.
Their smiles are glowing brightly
    They beam with sheer delight at my well-being.
I realise how lucky I am
    To have two people who care
        So very much.
I may suffer with my illness
    But they always show their love.
Now I am feeling well
    I can add it all up
        And realise I have more
            Than many people have.
            I have love.

                        Margaret

DAWN OVER EDEN

Inside a singular particularity,
The widest horizon I can see is inside my eye.
All I want to see is out of sight,
Where I want to be, somewhere, far removed.
Where I have been being darkness,
Where I want to be is bright.

It leaves me happy just to be in this place, A smile inside me constantly.

I will be bathed in warmth, light, comfort - I will be as light as air.

I am strong here, though weak and sensitive as ever.

Even if I put a foot wrong, it will not leave an indelible footprint, where people say,

"That's where she made her mistake and she never got any further"

"She never travelled anymore on her journey"

"Her life was frustrated at this point"

"Cut short, and we could never do any more to help her".

I will learn to speak in this place.
And I will learn to talk.

Anon

PERPETUAL DAWN

The day is over now
As she beckons
Calling, calling.
Sounds and colours
Magnify and surrounds
A vision so beautiful
Softer than the rain
Falling, falling
Harmonizing so mysteriously.

So I climb
The silver mountain
Over the crimson sea.
Thoughts cascading,
Passions weeping
Bringing chaos into meaning
Out of the void
Into reality.

Like the wild wind,
She calls, she calls
Perpetual dawn, perpetual dawn
As I whisper so quietly
To stand at the precipice
And fall into the sky.
Elixir of life
Elixir of life

For ashes to transcend
To watch the spirit fly.

C. McIntosh

THE BEAUTY OF NATURE

Today the sun is shining and the crocuses are out.
The daffodils have lifted themselves from beneath the ground.
How lucky are people who are blessed with good health.
Too many things are taken for granted
    And today at last, I join in with the appreciation of the
    beauty of nature.
Yesterday, it meant nothing, I only felt the cold chill of the wind
    And the bark of a tormented dog.
But today is beautiful and I feel at one with nature.
Life can be all worthwhile.
One day the clouds do pass over,
    The sun shines
        And a cat purrs.

Margaret

MY HILL

I have schizophrenia,
Restlessness is my plight.
I try hard to beat it
But it's an uphill fight.

If I begin to relax
I slide down the slope,
So i keep going
And live in hope.

Often the past is steep
But I cannot rest.
I must keep going
Until I reach the crest.

I must keep going
And never stop
Or I'll fall backwards
And never reach the top.

But someday I'll feel good
And no longer be ill
When I reach the summit
Of my personal hill.

Then I'll look around
And throw down some rope

To help other people
Climb up the slope.

Then knowing me,
Who can never rest,
I might just go and climb
Mount Everest!

Jim Wilson

11. SIR CLIFF RICHARD

11a - With Thanks

A FRIEND IN NEED

There used to be times of despair
    when I wondered, did anyone care?
I would sit and cry,
    'till I found no hanky was dry.
I was so alone.
No one could understand
    the pain and desperation I could feel, it was oh so very real.
No one could see into my world.
It took years for me to find
    I had friends and family, who were really kind.
I found along the way,
    someone who brought some light into my day.
        Cliff Richard would play his part,
            with songs that would soothe my aching heart.
He reached out with his love, and told me of the story
    that God cared and spoke of the glory.
Nothing can compare
    with the love that He displays
        it will keep me going through these days.
With my brother in God's keeping.
    I can rest, and one day I'll have peaceful sleeping.

Margaret

OH NO, NOT THAT CLIFF RICHARD!

What does she see in that Cliff Richard? Cliff is very special to me. When I am ill it feels as though the world is against me and madness reigns, that is when I know I can turn to Cliff. My faith is very important to me, as it is to him. Cliff is always there when I need him. I can see him on video and I can hear him when I play his music. He leads his life in a way that is an example to any Christian. I know that in my vulnerability I can put my trust in Cliff. When I am low, Cliff can convey God's love just by the way he leads his life.

I know I can depend on Cliff. To me Cliff sums up what true love really means. Love is the most precious gift that can be given. I know that when my world is turned upside down, and those that are near and care about me seem to be my enemies, love seems to turn to hate in my world. I know at this time I can turn to Cliff's love. It is safe, it is distant, it is what love really means. It engulfs me, sometimes it becomes too real, and I can begin to turn it into something personal and fantasy takes over. This is usually the point where I leave reality and end up in hospital, at which point I am disappointed that Cliff hasn't turned into my knight in shining armour, and eventually feet reach floor and I am in a safe environment in hospital.

Cliffs love has helped me; he has given me a blanket of security to cling on to when I need it. No harm done, just a slight case of embarrassment when reality dawns!

Margaret

SHARE A DREAM
ASWAD AND CLIFF RICHARD

Hey when you're feeling low
When the blues refuse to let you go
Just reach out for my hand
I can understand
Come share a dream with me

Hey love will find a way
It doesn't matter what the people say
Don't try to hide the way you really feel
Time can only heal
Come share a dream with me

We could rise above all the tears
All the doubts and the fears
We can make a stand here and now
Higher love
Got to learn to trust in a friend
For a peace without end
Oh come share a dream with me

Hey children of the world
Is the dream we're dreaming so absurd
Sweet reason's just a friendly smile away
'Cos love is here to stay
Come share a dream with me

We could rise above all the tears
All the doubts and the fears
We can make a stand here and now
Higher love
Got to learn to trust in a friend
For a peace without end
Oh come share a dream with me

We could build a castle so tall
Oh the thrill of it all
Won't you find a place in your heart?

We could rise above all the tears
All the doubts and the fears
We can make a stand here and now
Higher love
Got to learn to trust in a friend
For a peace without end
Oh come share a dream with me

Courtesy of: Patch Music/Peer Music
The words were a comfort to me when I was ill - Margaret

SHARE A DREAM

I find myself reminiscing,
    Remembering times of old.
A long old haul it has been,
But I had a friend who helped me through.
I would hear him sing with such emotion.
    I needed to escape, escape the pain.
I could 'Lean On You', and 'Share A Dream'.
    A castle we could all live in
I guess I am a romantic,
    But romance is not what I had in mind
        Just to be equal, just a love for God.

Margaret

TO CLIFF

I've been thinking, long and hard
Whether to send to you or discard
All the things I want to say:
(I know that they would make your day!)
Thanks, and more thanks for all you've done
In making my life a more happy one.
Words of wisdom, you display
Arms of muscles, when tennis you play.
I know you've heard it all before,
You're the best and that's for sure.
God and Jesus we adore
Thanks to you, He means so much more.
Through your life you show to me,
How God's light glows bright and free.
Thank you Cliff, what more can I say?
You're the best, to show us all the way.

Margaret

TO CLIFF

'Thank you' are two words often spoken,
　　But when they're said to you
　　　　It's clear to see
　　　　　　The thanks I feel are sincere from me.
They are sent to you
　　With much more meaning
　　　　Than mere words can express.
The extent of the joy I feel is such,
　　That if I can feel there is any pain,
　　　　It is soothed with just the mention of your name.

Margaret

WHEN CLIFF SINGS

When Cliff sings
  I can believe it's meant just for me.
I can be Sarah, Joanna or Carrie.
I can enter a fantasy Island
  And hear the emotion in his voice.
When manic depression takes its grip,
  And my nearest and dearest
    Seem so distant, even though they are close.
I look for love, from a distant friend.
  Someone who cares, and cares for all.
I feel his love, and it fills that need.
I can always feel that love,
  But mostly when I am in need,
    He is always a special friend to me.

Margaret

Lightning Source UK Ltd.
Milton Keynes UK
UKOW06f0609070217
293785UK00011B/731/P